The Art of Brazilian Cookery

The Art of Brazilian Cookery

Dolores Botafogo

HIPPOCRENE BOOKS
New York

Originally published by Doubleday & Company, New York.
Hippocrene Paperback Edition, 1993.
Third Printing, 1999
Cover photograph© Madeline Polss.

For information, address:
HIPPOCRENE BOOKS, INC.
171 Madison Avenue
New York, NY 10016

ISBN 0-7818-0130-3

Printed in the United States of America.

CONTENTS

Recipes capitalized in the text may be located
by consulting the Index

THE ART OF BRAZILIAN COOKERY

INTRODUCTION

This sun, this moon,
These rivers, these waterfalls,
Flowers and the sea
And a world of palm trees,
All this is mine, my Brazil.
God gave it to me.
He must be a Brazilian,
Brazilian as am I!

From the song "Minha Terra,"
words and music by Waldemar Henrique.

It is intensely exciting to see the lands of the Southern Cross for the first time—that vast region of dense tropical forests hardly explored or even penetrated; turbulent, legendary rivers where the volume of water is so great and so spectacular that the sea itelf seems to be compressed between their banks. Trees blossoming in masses of purple, red, and yellow, and others with leaves of silvery white, break into the dense green foliage of the forests. There are brilliant blue skies and waters, mountains, waterfalls, lakes, prairie, and caatinga (desert-like land of weird beauty covered with sparse vegetation). There are mountains and highlands with warm days and cold nights; in the south there is frost and even ice in the winter. Large areas are steamy hot most of the year, but unvarying cool winds make parts of the coast delightful the year round.

In the great cities, architecture of four centuries ago stands beside the daring creations of famous modern architects, pointing to the future that is just beginning. Here are schools and universities, art museums, concert halls and theaters, football games, yachting, bathing on white beaches, interesting religious processions on the *avenidas,* and *macumba* (voodoo) back in the hills. Pretty, slim girls are chic in lovely clothes or comfortable in blue jeans and low heels. Colored women carry huge bundles on their heads, and peddlers sell ice cream, candy, popcorn, and soft drinks.

This immense country, one of the largest in the world, is Brazil. Its people, of mixed blood, are welcoming and warm. Their music, whether it be a legendary tune of the Amazon, a *candomblé* (ritualistic voodoo chant from Bahia), a cowboy melody from Rio Grande, the popular sentimental samba, or the *rodas* (musical games) sung by the children in the park—all have a simple, plaintive, rhythmic quality, at once sad and happy. Just as the music definitely depicts national customs and characteristics, so the culinary art, extremely savory and varied, reflects the genius of all the people who make up the population of this far-flung country.

Brazilians are perhaps as mixed a people as the Americans of the United States. Brazil was first settled in 1531 by the Portuguese and was under Portuguese rule until 1822, when it declared its independence and was ruled by the first emperor, Dom Pedro I. It became a republic in 1889. French and Dutch were among the first European settlers on the northeastern coast. Later the Dutch were driven out, but some of their fair-haired descendants are still to be seen in that region. Many of the Brazilian people are descended from the native Indians and the Africans who came as slaves in the early days. In colonial times in the north, and in what is now the state of Rio de Janeiro, Brazil was a country of vast sugar plantations, with coffee plantations in the state of São Paulo. With their great houses and slave quarters, these plantation owners may be compared with the southern aristocracy in the United States. The patriarchal "big house" was the center of life: fort, factory, school, hospital, convent for the girls, hotel, and even bank.

Bands of hardy pioneers (*bandeirantes*) went out from São Paulo into the vast hinterland to the west. Gold was discovered in what is now Minas Gerais, as well as semiprecious stones, aquamarines, amethysts, tourmalines, precious topaz, and even diamonds. In the old town of Ouro Prêto (now in the state of Minas Gerais), the many churches were richly decorated with the plentiful gold, and it was woven into the priests' vestments, which are today carefully guarded in old chests. It is worth traveling many hours to see these treasures and the beautiful images sculptured by the son of slaves, the Aleijadinho (the Little Crippled One). Here too is the museum which guards the relics of the days when Ouro Prêto was the birthplace of Brazilian independence and where Joaquim José da Silva Xavier, called "Tiradentes," (the Tooth Puller—he was a dentist) was hanged, a martyr in the cause of his country's freedom. This wide inland country (today the states of Minas Gerais, São Paulo, Paraná, and parts of Mato Grosso) is rich with large cattle ranches, plantations of coffee and cotton, sugar cane, mandioca, rice, beans, and fruit. Iron ore and other minerals are mined in Minas Gerais and have helped in the great industrial development of Brazil.

In the nineteenth century, immigrants came from other European countries; Germans, Italians, and Poles settled in the south and started great industries in the city of São Paulo. There was even a small group of Americans from the southern states, who came after the Civil War. They hoped to be able to carry on in Brazil with their plantations and slaves. They have retained their identity with their American names, and speak English with a bit of a southern accent. Among genuine Brazilian family names are found the Dodsworths, Kellys, Archers, MacDowells, and others— from the English, Scots, and Irish settlers who have become part of the Brazilian people. The Syrians and the Lebanese have contributed greatly to the development of industries in Brazil, with their skill in business, as well as in the professions and in politics. They have come by the thousands and settled all over Brazil, in the small towns as well as the large cities. More recently have come the displaced persons and refugees from Europe, first those fleeing from Nazi Germany, and, later, those from the Iron Curtain countries. Japanese immigrants, with their skill in horticulture, help to supply the large centers of population with fresh vegetables. Even with all this conglomeration of peoples, Portuguese, spoken with a Brazilian accent, is the national language, interspersed with many words of Indian, African, French, and English origin.

The capital of Brazil is Rio de Janeiro, the "Marvelous City," as it is called by its poets and singers; and certainly it is one of the most beautiful cities of the world. Whether seen from the air or from the sea, the panoramic view is a spectacle of brilliant light and color and physical contours of surprising majesty. A new capital, Brasília, is being audaciously built in the countryside in the heart of Brazil, in the state of Goiás. Planned by the most famous Brazilian architects, it has already brought to this side of the Atlantic personalities most distinguished in the world of art, business, and politics.

When you take a plane southward bound, your first stop in Brazil will be Belém do Pará. Belém is on the Amazon River, where it meets the ocean on the north coast of Brazil. You will find the climate very hot. Walking along the streets, shaded with large, spreading, dark green tropical trees, seeing the fine old residences, one is reminded of the earlier days, when all the ladies' gowns were brought from Paris, and French culture was predominant. In those days, it is said, the ruffled white shirts of the gentlemen of the great houses were sent by sailing ships to France to be laundered. Today in Belém, the laundress takes your clothes and brings them back snowy and starched and faintly perfumed with the resins from tropical trees.

In your hotel you may dine in a charming, open-air patio, and the daily rain shower will have freshened the air and brought out the perfume of the tropical vegetation. It is here that you will first taste Brazilian cooking. Many of the regional dishes are of native Indian origin. The first settlers found the Indians living by hunting and fishing and eating the fruit that hung so lavishly from the trees. They knew how to prepare food lovely to the taste, as well as strong drink—a taste for which should be acquired slowly. The whole Amazon region, which comprises the immense states of Amazonas and Pará and part of the north of Mato Grosso, abounds with tropical fruits and fish, which to this day form a large part of the daily diet of the inhabitants. In Belém you will find the famous Pato no Tucupi (Duck with Tucupi Sauce). You may savor a drink called *tacacá*, which, in the centuries-old tradition, is sold in lovely bowls by slender quadroons wearing wide skirts

and using those same exotic perfumes which the laundress uses to perfume your clothes. The "scented" quadroon is one of the delightful types who contribute to the charm of the city of Nossa Senhora de Belém do Pará (Our Lady of Bethlehem of Pará).

In the morning, women go from house to house, selling Cuscuz, a kind of molded pudding made of toasted manioc flour, saturated with coconut milk, sprinkled with grated coconut, and then folded into a banana leaf. You will soon acquire a taste for this delightful mixture.

Delectable sweets are made from the Pará nut (Brazil nut). The tree which bears this nut is one of the most beautiful of the tropical forests, and sometimes reaches a height of 250 feet. Fish cookery in the north of Brazil is an art that blends the flavors of fish, shellfish, coconut, and other ingredients into dishes that are delightfully strange and delicious. Here is the *pirarucú* (a species of tropical codfish) and the *muçuá*, which is the kind of turtle preferred at the feasts of the interior tableland. The flesh of this small turtle is minced and baked in its own carapace. There is *açai*, a crushed mixture of the fruit of the *açai* palm. Where *açai* is sold, they hang out a red flag. Should you want to make some, soak the fruit in hot water or leave it in the sun in a wooden bowl with a curved bottom. Then, capped and aproned, manipulate the fruit so that in rubbing it against the bottom of the bowl, its pulp is released. Your hands become dyed a deep red as you work. Add water as necessary until a thick liquid can be taken off. This is served in small bowls with sugar and manioc or tapioca flour. A little lemon juice will remove the red color from your hands completely. Traditionally, *açai* is supposed to be the supreme delight in Pará and Amazonas. The popular verse runs:

> "Who visits Pará is glad to stay,
> Who drinks *açai* never goes away."

Look on your map for Recife, in the state of Pernambuco, which lies on the Atlantic coast almost at the point of the great hump. Here you will probably stop at a hotel on the beach. In the city it is very hot, but along the beaches there is always a fresh breeze, which rustles the leaves of the thousands of palm trees. Fragile-seeming *jangadas* (fishing rafts) toss on the waves. With their white sails on the brilliant blue-green water, they seem to have been put there to make a charming picture. The *jangadas* are made of very light, soft wood, shaped and lashed together almost as if they were only hastily improvised for temporary use—but their sails can take them sixty or a hundred miles from the shore, and from three to five men spend many days fishing, cooking their meals, and sleeping aboard, without coming close to the land.

Homes in Recife are comfortable and have deep verandas full of ornamental plants. Bright flowering vines cover the houses, and the gardens are beautifully cared for and rich with the color of tropical blooms. Appetizing fragrances come from the kitchens, where the shrimp and corn dishes for which this region is famous are prepared: the Camarão Com Chuchu (Shrimp with Chayote) and Tigelinhas de Milho Verde—"little saucers of green corn" (Corn and Coconut Pudding). The diet is varied with vegetables and every kind of fruit, but black beans and rice are always on the table, as in all Brazilian homes. As you walk along the beach, you will find many delicious fruits to buy, as well as green coconut. You scoop out the pulp of green coconut and eat it with a spoon.

The small state of Maranhão joins Amazonas on its eastern border, and there you will want to stop briefly to eat the delicious Shrimp Pie. This is made of fresh and dried shrimp, with seasonings and potatoes, and baked in the oven with eggs, a kind of omelet.

There has been some Arabian influence in the food of northeastern Brazil, especially in sweets and drinks, but for the most part the food is similar to that of Pará, with fish and shellfish predominating.

> "My love, have you been to Bahia?
> No? Then go, go, go!
> There you will find *carurú*,
> V*atapá* is there too,
> So go, go, go."

Dorival Caymi, one of Brazil's popular entertainers, wrote and sings this song, of his own beautiful Bahia. You will want to stop in the city of São Salvador, one of the most ancient in Brazil. It is a city of three hundred and sixty-five churches, of sloping streets, of *candomblé*, of coconut palms swaying in the wind, of beaches, of fishing boats, of singers, and of poets. The beauty of this region is revealed gradually, day by day, when living there in intimacy with its people. The dark, vivacious, fascinating Carmen Miranda, film and night-club star, personified so well the charm of Bahia. With her typical Bahiana costume, wide skirts, beads and *balangandãs* (bangles), and basket of fruit tilted on her head, she reminded us of those exotic dishes, Vatapá, Acarajé, and Carurú. Contrary to Belém do Pará, Salvador, the capital of the state of Bahia, has culinary specialties brought from Africa by the Negroes who became the slaves on the great plantations. The semibarbaric dishes of the Negroes were of exquisite flavor and considerable nutritive value. Today, versions of these dishes are so relished that composers sometimes set music to verses in praise of the marvels of local cookery.

Carurú is a dish of Sudanese origin, which has fish as a basis. The name, however, is clearly of the Tupi Indian tongue. It is prepared with *quiabos* (okra) and served with rice, *aberém*, or *acaçá*. *Aberém* is made of corn meal, which is ground on stones, with some sugar and with coconut milk to moisten, wrapped in specially prepared banana leaves, and steamed. *Acaçá* is made of corn meal previously fermented in water, mixed with coconut milk, and boiled in banana leaves. Corn prepared in various ways is always present on the table of the Bahiano, rich or poor. Corn meal and flour, hominy and fresh green corn are used for cakes, other desserts, and as accompaniment to different dishes. Corn is so important as a food that it carries special virtues, and it is said that when a kettle is slow in coming to a boil, adding three grains of corn will make it boil immediately. Acarajé is a cake made from beans, with a sauce of onions, shrimp, and *malagueta* pepper. The beans are soaked in cold water until the skins can be removed, then grated and stirred to a paste, adding salt and grated onion. *Dendê* oil from the *dendê* palm is heated in a clay frying pan and, with a wooden spoon, small blobs of paste are added and rolled around in the frying pan with a fork until the paste is cooked and has become the color of the oil. World-famous is the Afro-Brazilian Vatapá. Fish or shellfish is mixed in a kind of porridge made from manioc flour with *dendê* oil, coconut milk, and some or a great deal of pepper. Some types include meat or chicken. It is said that it was originally prepared by the Nupés Negroes and adopted by the Iorubas tribe, who brought it to Bahia under the name of "Enbá-Tapá."

Perhaps more than in any other place in Brazil, cookery in Bahia is a tradition and an art that is interwoven with the folklore of the country. I am indebted to Hildegardes Víanna's charming book, A Cozinha Bahiana (Fundação Gonçalo Moniz: 1955) for the following discussion of some of the numerous superstitions surrounding the activities of the kitchen and the eating habits of the people.

Rich and poor alike are devoted to the old order of procedure in the kitchen—for example, "Good beans are cooked only in a clay pot." And whether the roof of the kitchen be of straw, tiles, or the concrete blocks of modern construction, the children still throw the tooth which has just been extracted onto the roof, saying:

"Mourão, Mourão, take your old tooth and give me a nice new one!" (Mourão is a proper name and has no significance.)

The kitchen stove, excepting the modern ones (oil, gas, or electricity), is built of clay and tiles, with an iron oven and a space underneath where pots and pans, or wood may be kept. This space is sometimes used as a brooder for baby chicks. And even in the modern kitchen there is always the iron fogareiro, a small charcoal-burning stove or hot plate, as well as an infinity of utensils on the shelves: iron grills, wooden spoons, fire tongs, and so forth, and a collection of cans and bottles containing various kinds of oil, preserved hot peppers, and all the seasonings, plus the coffee-pot and cloth bag for making the coffee. Hanging near the chimney are the bunches of bay leaves and other herbs used for seasoning; the medicinal herbs; and a basket holding onions and garlic. Then there is the inevitable braided fan of bright straw, which is indispensable for fanning the fire. The Bahianos say that when the wind blows, or when the fire crackles and snaps as it is fanned, it is a sign that money and prosperity will come to the head of the house. When the tide is high, the fire catches easily, but when it is at ebb, the fire will burn only when fanned vigorously.

A picture of the image of St. Benedict may be found hanging on the walls of the kitchen—which are blackened by the smoke of the fire and the kerosene lamp used for illumination—because St. Benedict in the kitchen is said to guarantee a plentiful supply of food. A large clay pot, with the classic coconut shell—or the more modern dipper—holds the water. This pot is kept very clean: the water is changed frequently, and the receptacle is covered with a snowy cloth. Even in the more up-to-date kitchens there is always a clay pot, into which water filters directly from a conveniently placed faucet. The large sieves and strainers, sometimes woven of vegetable fiber, hang right outside the kitchen door, next to the parrot's perch. The spoons are always of wood, sometimes with decorated handles which are too beautiful to use, from which comes the saying: "He who has too much time on his hands makes a spoon and carves the handle." When the spoons get old, they are used to stir up the fire. It is said to be bad luck to put a knife in the fire, except in cases of a wound caused by a nail, when the knife is heated to pat on the wounded place until "you feel the blood spreading." Speaking of nails, if you stick the nail that caused the injury into a fresh onion, the wound will not become infected.

The Bahiana knows that if many people stir the cooking pot, the food will come out either insipid or too salty, and that any dish which has to be cooked to an exact thickness will not come out well if stirred by two people. When you cook rice, if you want it to cook light and fluffy, fill your cheeks with air at the exact moment that the rice starts to boil. And do not beat the wooden spoon on the edge of the pot, or the rice is sure to burn.

Food cooked in clay pots and vessels is thought to be of incomparable flavor, and despite modern cooking utensils, this material is used in all Bahian kitchens. The pots used in making *canjica* (corn dessert) and fine sweets are of smoother texture, and every family has its cooking vessels, wooden spoons, and sieves reserved for such use. The care of these cooking utensils is almost a ritual. (If a wooden spoon is left resting on the lid of a boiling kettle, it causes an enormous amount of trouble, it is believed. The kitchen will always be in disorder, and the food in the kettles will not cook tender.)

If you are cooking food with oil, it is a good idea to toss a little of it outside the kitchen door into the grass or bushes, "for the boys." The "boys" are the twin saints, Cosme and Damion. They say it is bad luck to step on ashes that have fallen from the stove; there is sure to arise some great confusion or quarrel. And if a visitor stays too long, and wears out his welcome, stick an old, worn-

down knife in an onion, and the visitor will leave, "as if by magic."
You can also get rid of an unwelcome visitor by standing the broom
upside down in back of the door, with the floor cloth on top
of it, and saying, "Mr. So-and-So, take your hat and go."

Fly down to the southern part of Brazil to the prairies of Rio
Grande do Sul, the land of the *churrasco* (barbecue). Here are
vast *estancias* (cattle ranches), plantations of rice, wheat, and
other cereals. Because of his nomadic life, the food of the *gaúcho*
(cowboy) is meat, eaten with manioc flour, and *chimarrão* (tea
made of the mate herb). Since there are beef cattle in abundance,
it is possible to kill a steer every day for food. When the *gaúchos*
have to go long distances on horseback, the easiest thing to carry is
meat and salt, since water and wood for making the fire are always
available. Even though there may be drought during the summer
months, there is always water in the rivers and streams.

The *gaúcho* is a distinctive type, happy and full of life. He loves
to sing the story of his life in verse, accompanied by the *violão*,
(mandolin), drinking *chimarrão* beside the fire. *Chimarrão* is the
first thing taken in the morning, before the first cigarette, and it
is also taken at meals and intervals during the day. It is the "pipe
of peace" of the *gaúcho*; for when a stranger or visitor appears, he
is offered not the traditional Brazilian coffee but *chimarrão* served
from a common *cúia* and common *bomba* (tube). The *cúia* is made
of a hollowed-out gourd, which is polished and dried and sometimes elaborately trimmed with silver. The iron tea kettle is kept
boiling over the fire, the *cúia* filled almost to the top with the
mate, water poured in, the tube inserted—and then it is offered to
the first partaker. It is very bitter at first, but as the *cúia* is refilled
with hot water and passed around the circle, the *chimarrão* becomes weaker. The *gaúchos* are a picturesque lot, with their wide
bombachas (pantaloons), big hats, boots, and ponchos. The pon-
cho is an almost square blanket with a slit in the middle large
enough to allow it to slip over the head. It can be very luxurious
and beautiful, woven of fine wool, and it is a protection from the
cold rain and wind. Winter is the rainy season, and it gets cold
enough to freeze a coating of ice on the puddles. In some places
there is sometimes a light fall of snow.

In the cities and towns, the "*gaúchos*" have a more varied diet (the people of Rio Grande do Sul are all called *"gaúchos,"* whether they are cowboys or not). They have wheat bread, corn meal, and other cereals, rice and beans, vegetables, meat and fruits. There are grapes in abundance, and the delicious Rio Grande wines are shipped all over Brazil and to foreign countries. There are all kinds of citrus fruits, figs, and even apples and peaches. American visitors to Rio Grande who know its life and customs are reminded of their own great state of Texas.

In the southern state of Santa Catarina, in addition to the Brazilian rice and beans and other staple Brazilian foods, the German influence is shown in the cold suppers that are served, consisting of pumpernickel, cold meats, sausages and cheeses of various types, pickles, and a delicious dessert of tapioca cooked in grape juice. Coffee with milk, strong and hot, accompanies this cold meal. In Santa Catarina, as well as in Rio Grande, German is spoken by many of these German Brazilians, and even by the native Brazilians who have come in contact with the German-speaking people.

In Rio de Janeiro, São Paulo, and all through the great middle states, the everyday food of the people is rice, beans, meat, manioc flour, bread, fruit, vegetables, and many dishes made of corn and macaroni. Here the diet approaches the international type of food, with accents of the regional and more exotic dishes. The housewife in the large cities buys her vegetables and fruit at the street markets. She takes her cook with her to push the cart carrying home the purchases, but she also likes to go to the supermarkets, where she waits on herself, as do American housewives.

In the small interior towns and on the farms and ranches, the rhythm of life is simpler and slower than in the large cities. Brazilians are an air-minded people, and you can go by plane to the very edge of civilization, and even fly over the jungle, which is inhabited by Indians completely isolated from the modern world. They have been known to shoot their arrows at planes that have come close to them.

If you are willing to stand a little discomfort, you can travel on one of the interior trains, which jog along, stopping at every station. When the train stops, small boys run along the side, selling their fruit, *empadas* (meat-filled pies), various small cakes made of corn meal or manioc flour, lengths of sugar cane to suck, or *garapa* (a drink made of crushed sugar cane). There is every variety of banana. You have not eaten bananas until you have eaten the sweet, melt-in-the-mouth delicacy of Brazil. It is not necessary to pick them as green and hard as those that are exported, which is probably the reason for their superior flavor and texture. There is beautiful *mamão* (papaya) to be bought, and you may see clusters of them hanging from the tree, seeming almost too heavy for the slender stem. There may be piles of *cajú* (cashew), delicate, yellow in color, and so full of juice that it may run down your chin as you eat. The shelled and toasted nut is the cashew that is served in North America. On the tree, the nut hangs as though it were an afterthought, from the flower end of the fruit. There may be baskets of mangoes, or the small, shiny, dark red *jaboticaba*. The *jaboticaba* fruit clings almost like a fungus growth, directly to the bark of the tree. Where they are plentiful, you can go to an orchard, "buy" a tree for the day, and have as many as you can eat or carry away.

In the meantime, as you journey along, your neighbor across the aisle opens his lunch. He is a *caipira* (simple person of the interior). He most certainly has smiled and said "Good morning" to you as you got on the train, and would not think of eating without asking you, a perfect stranger, to share his food with him. He will probably have a thick sandwich of bread with country cheese or sausage, a package of *farofa* (a manioc-flour preparation), or some "cake" made of *fubá* (corn meal).

You get off the train and a car carries you to a *fazenda* (ranch), where you are hospitably received by the *fazendeiro* (rancher) and his family in their comfortable home. The house may date from the old colonial days, with its veranda running around three or four sides of the house, cool and inviting, with the overhanging flowering vines and thick shrubbery. You relax in the shade, dreamily taking in the beauty of the scene before you—perhaps rolling pastures, splashed with brilliant flowering trees, palms, or a bit of the jungle, and some distant blue mountains. You smell the gordura grass (a rich native grass excellent for fattening cattle) and the faint moist sweetness that comes with the breeze off the great green jungles. You see the flash of brilliant parakeets in the air and hear the squawk of the arara, that large brilliant macaw, so much more beautiful to see than to hear. In the cool dining room, you sit down with the family and other guests at the big table and are served by a maid dressed in a clean cotton print dress and apron. Possibly she is barefoot. There are large dishes of rice and black beans; stewed okra or other vegetables; beef cut and fried in thin slices; Ensopado de Galinha (chicken stewed with tomatoes, onions, and potatoes); a platter of fried eggs or an omelet; and you finish with a *pudim de caramelo* (rich custard baked with caramelized sugar) or homemade guava paste served with fresh white cheese. Finally come the small cups of thick, sweet coffee. Later you may be offered Cocadas (coconut candies) or fruit candied in thick syrup.

Your *fazendeiro* friend shows you around the *fazenda*, and you drop in to the adobe hut of one of his workers. These are simple people, but they are pleased to have you visit them in their home, and they receive you with gentle dignity. Again you are served coffee in a little cup, this time sweetened with *rapadura* (dark brown sugar). The well-behaved, dark-eyed, brown-skinned children sit quietly, greatly interested in their visitor. Later on, when the sun is low, you leave the *fazenda*, perhaps loaded with a whole stem of bananas, fresh manioc roots, oranges, guavas or pineapples, or some candied figs or other fruits—or, if you are staying in Brazil, a potted plant or some slips to plant in your garden. You will have no trouble making them grow in this country where the telephone poles along rural roads sometimes sprout a thick leafy growth from their tips.

In the large cities the food is more cosmopolitan, both in the homes and in hotels and restaurants. There are all kinds of eating places, French, Italian, Syrian, Polish, German, Hungarian, Chinese, Japanese, and others serving an international type of food with some regional dishes. There are beautiful, luxurious restaurants as well as bars, stand-up eating places, where hot dogs, cheeseburgers, soft drinks, and ice-cream cones are sold. There are ice-cream bars, where the specialties are the delicious ices and sherbets made of tropical fruits—*cajú, maracujá,* mango, avocado, and pineapple. There are the tearooms, where you pass a pleasant hour having tea and perhaps watching a birthday party. Children, relatives, and friends are seated at a long table, where they are served thin sandwiches, tiny shrimp and chicken croquettes, Empadinhas (little pies of shrimp, chicken, or codfish), Coxinhas (legs of chicken wrapped in a creamy paste, breaded, and fried), delightfully decorated small cakes, soft drinks, pastel-colored ice creams, and, last, the beautiful birthday cake with candles—accompanied by the orchestra playing "Happy Birthday," while beaming grown-ups watch the little guest of honor blow out the candles.

> "Parabens para você,
> Nesta data querida,
> Muitas felicidades
> Muitos anos de vida."

This is the Brazilian song of congratulation, sung to the tune of "Happy Birthday to You." In Brazilian homes every kind of anniversary, christening, or first communion is an excuse for a *festa*. There is even a *festa* when the roof is put on a new house, and the workmen and owners drink beer and soft drinks and eat sandwiches and sweets to celebrate this happy occasion. It is not unusual to see, high up on some tall building in the city, the leafy branches that they use to decorate the construction for this *festa*. To the parties at home, everyone is invited, grandmas and grandpas, aunts, uncles, cousins, godparents, friends of all ages. Grown-ups as well as children celebrate birthdays. Children often are allowed to stay out of school on their birthdays. Everyone comes to give the honored one an *abraço* (embrace). Congratulations and good wishes are offered not only to the happy celebrant but also to parents and godparents, with the exchange of many endearing expressions and kisses on both cheeks. The *mesa de doçes* (table of sweets) is wonderful to see—a beautiful cake in a marvelous shape, intricately decorated, appropriate to the occasion; baskets, bowls, and plates of various sweets, beautifully wrapped in silver and gold paper or fringed tissue and cellophane; candies hidden in the stems of soft-colored tissue flowers. There may be Olhos de Sogra, Casadinhos, Brigadeiros, Quindins, and Mãe Bentas. Small sandwiches are passed, and tiny bite-size croquettes, sizzling hot, squares of beef fillet toasted on toothpicks, fried shrimp, and flaky cheese tidbits. Soft drinks and punch are served, with perhaps something stronger for the adults. And always there is the tray of piping hot *cafézinhos* (demitasse). The "small fry" enjoy this repast as much as the grown-ups. They perhaps will enjoy a movie

23

in another part of the house, while the grown-ups exchange gossip, admire babies, talk about the servant problem and the high cost of living.

Dona Dolores Botafogo, Brazilian lady, expert cook, charming hostess, and loving friend, is the personification of the Brazilian spirit. Many years ago, by chance, she attended a class in cake decoration, and since that time, cooking has been her pastime and her profession. Full of energy, she is never too busy to teach a beginner the mysteries of Massa Folheada (Puff Paste) or the intricate decoration of a special cake, or to give a cooking demonstration on television. Between all these activities and the compilation of four enormous cookbooks, she still has time to prepare delicious *quitutes* (delightful delicacies) for her family and to prepare for you this collection of recipes, adapted for use in the American kitchen.

GRETCHEN ORCUTT

TO MY READERS

There are many things that I would like to tell you about my people. With you we share love for our homes and children and have many of the same problems of everyday life. Brazilian wives and mothers are concerned with the health and well-being of their families, and many hours of the day are spent in the planning and preparation of food. Aside from the daily routine of family duties, we enjoy the company of our friends, and some of our happiest hours are spent in preparing for the guests who visit us in our homes.

To make the friendship between our two countries stronger, I offer you dishes which will remind you of Brazil, its customs, and its cordial and kindly people. Some may seem strange to you, but their preparation will be like a cooking adventure in a foreign country and perhaps they may become family favorites and thus be incorporated into North American cookery. Prepare them with love and care and think of this great country to the south as you serve them to your family and friends.

DOLORES BOTAFOGO

about BRAZILIAN RECIPES

The word *refogado* is used extensively in these recipes, and denotes the basic process of practically all Brazilian cooking. There is no English equivalent, so the Portuguese word has been retained. It means lightly sautéing onion, or garlic, or both, or tomato, in a little cooking fat, cooking slowly, and often adding other ingredients.

Thick coconut milk is used in many Brazilian recipes. It may be obtained in food specialty stores, in cans or bottles. One can or bottle usually holds about ¾ cup. If this is not available, you may grind fresh coconut in the blender (after the dark skin is removed), or grate it, and then press out the juice through a cloth. One coconut has about ½ cup of very thick milk. Water may be added to the coconut to obtain more milk, but it will be thinner. If a recipe calls for ¾ cup, you will probably get enough milk from 1 coconut, with a little of the thinner juice added. If fresh coconut is not available, use a can of vacuum-packed coconut, soaked in 1½ cups hot water for several hours. Then press out all the juice. If you have any thin coconut juice left after preparing one of these recipes, you can use it in cooking plain rice, or add powdered milk and sugar to make a delicious drink.

Dried shrimps are available in specialty food stores, but if you do not find them, use an equal amount of canned, dry-pack shrimp (or, if they are not available, frozen shrimp could be substituted). Dry out the shrimp in a slow oven, and proceed according to the recipe, and the result will be perfect. If the dried shrimps have shells, soak for a while in warm water to facilitate shelling. Taste these dishes for salt; small quantities have been indicated because of the difference in materials used.

Manioc flour is a coarse flour made from the roots of the *mandioca* plant, from which tapioca also is made. Farina or dry, fine-rolled bread crumbs may be substituted, according to the recipe.

Dendê oil is a vegetable oil used in northern Brazilian dishes. It is very hard to find in the United States, but corn or peanut oil may be substituted for it.

Cachaça, a native Brazilian rum made from sugar cane, is clear in color and potent. Rum is probably the best substitute.

The times for preparing coconut milk, drying shrimp, preparing dry bread crumbs, cleaning shrimp (except in recipes that call for the shells and heads of shrimp for broth), and hardening gelatin or other molds in the refrigerator, have not been included in the preparation times of these recipes. Using frozen or canned shrimp, or canned coconut milk, will of course reduce the preparation times considerably.

APPETIZERS

In Brazil we serve a variety of *salgadinhos* (literally, "salty things"), which include hors d'oeuvres, canapés, and sandwiches, at our parties and other *festas*. Served on our best crystal and silver plates, the table covered with handmade lace and embroidered cloths, with an arrangement of leaves and tropical blossoms as a centerpiece, they are indeed a mouth-watering sight. If the occasion celebrates a birthday or other anniversary, the house will be full of flowers which friends have sent.

Many kinds of canapés and croquettes are brought piping hot from the kitchen. You housewives in the United States who do all your own housework may not have time to make such a variety, but do try some of our appetizers at your next party as accompaniment to cocktails or served as hors d'oeuvres. The delicate Caviar Shells (Recipe 14) strike a luxurious note, but these pastry shells are different and equally delicious filled with any tasty mixture, such as finely chopped chicken or shrimp salad. Hot Cheese Puffs (Recipe 18) will disappear as if by magic. Plaza Prunes (Recipe 24), which are large prunes stuffed with cheese and peanuts, served in tiny paper cups, are unusual and easy to prepare. "Drumsticks" (Recipe 29) may be prepared ahead of time and fried as you need them. Crusty and hot, they are delicious as appetizers; served with a salad, they could be used as a luncheon dish the next time you entertain your bridge club.

Make a note of the Puffy Cheese Empadinha (Recipe 30), which can be served hot as an appetizer, or as a luncheon dish when made in larger sizes.

1. PUFF PASTRY (Massa Folheada)

Puff Pastry is the basis of many delicious canapés, patties, and desserts. I am giving you detailed instructions for making this dainty pastry. It may seem complicated to you at first, but with a little practice, you will make it quickly and easily.

First day: ½ hour; Second day: 1 hour

First part:

¾ cup flour
2¼ cups butter (unsalted if possible)

Sift the flour and work it into the butter until it is a smooth paste. Form it into a block about 6×8×2 inches; put it into the freezer for at least ½ hour.

Second part:

3 cups flour
1½ tablespoons salt (½ tablespoon if butter is salted)
1½ tablespoons butter
30 vol-au-vents

Sift flour and salt together, work in butter, and add enough cold water to make a rather soft dough, kneading it on a floured board until it does not stick to the fingers. Set aside, covered with a cloth.

Remove first part from the freezer (it should be hard to the touch). Roll out second part on a lightly floured board, to about 15×15 inches square, place the block (first part) in the center of second part, fold the four sides over it, from front to back, from back to front, from left to right, from right to left. With the rolling pin, pat this mass lightly, from front to back, from side to side, until it flattens somewhat. If it should break, and the butter mixture comes through, flour the broken part lightly. Then roll this paste into a long strip, about 18 inches, the strip going at right angles from the edge of table, or away from you. Fold this strip twice, so that each folded section is ⅓ of the strip and you have a square of about 6 inches.

Turn the dough so that the open edges are toward you, and again roll a long strip, fold again, wrap this in a dry napkin covered with a damp napkin, and put into the refrigerator for 2 hours. Then put it on the board again and repeat the rolling and folding process 2 times, then fold it together again and place it in a tightly covered dish and leave it in the refrigerator. The next day, repeat the process of rolling, folding, and turning twice, put in the refrigerator for 20 minutes, and again repeat.

Now the paste is ready to use. Cut off as much as you need and return the rest to the refrigerator, always tightly covered. The dough will keep for 6 or 8 days. Roll the dough to about ⅛ inch in thickness, cut in triangles or any desired shape, or in rounds not bigger than 2 inches in diameter.

2. VICTORY FILLING (Mistura Vitoria)

½ hour

2 tablespoons butter
3 tablespoons flour
1 cup cream
2 eggs
salt
pepper
3 tablespoons grated Parmesan cheese
1 tablespoon scraped onion
6 green olives, finely chopped
2 cups ground roasted veal or cooked ham, or finely cut up cooked chicken
garlic powder (optional)
24 portions

Melt the butter in a double boiler, mix in flour, slowly add cream, and cook until thick. Beat eggs, add a little of the cream mixture and mix well, put back into the double boiler, and cook for 2 minutes, stirring constantly. Add salt and pepper to taste, cheese, onion, and chopped olives. Stir in cooked meat. Add a little garlic powder if you wish. Cool.

31

3. VICTORY CANAPÉS (Canapé Vitoria)

45 minutes

24 biscuits made of Puff Pastry (Recipe 1) or 24 salted crackers
1 basic recipe Victory Filling (Recipe 2)
4 hard-cooked eggs, sliced
24 tomato slices
mayonnaise
cranberry jelly
water cress leaves
24 canapés

Make 24 patties with the Victory Filling, ⅛ inch thick and the same size as biscuits or crackers. Place them on top of biscuits; cover with slices of egg. Cut tomatoes in star shapes, put on top, and spread with mayonnaise. Put under broiler until hot. Garnish with dab of cranberry jelly and 2 or 3 water cress leaves.

4. STUFFED EGGS (Ovos Recheados)

45 minutes

24 biscuits made of Puff Pastry (Recipe 1), or 24 salted crackers
12 hard-cooked eggs
¼ teaspoon curry powder
salt
3 tablespoons soft butter
24 tomato slices
mayonnaise
24 capers
24 canapés

Cut the eggs in two, remove yolks, and mash with curry powder, salt to taste, and butter. Refill whites. Put a slice of tomato on each biscuit, cover with mayonnaise, put egg half on top, add another dab of mayonnaise and a caper.

32

5. BAHIA CANDLE   (Vela Baiana)

    35 minutes

24 biscuits made of Puff Pastry (Recipe 1), or 24 salted crackers
lettuce
mayonnaise
1 basic recipe Victory Filling (Recipe 2)
24 1-inch pieces of celery heart
24 pimento bits
    24 canapés

Put a piece of lettuce on each biscuit or cracker and spread with
mayonnaise. Make patties of Victory Filling and put on top of
lettuce, stick in a small piece of celery for the candle, with a bit
of pimento for flame.

6. VICTORY CROQUETTES (Croquetes Vitoria)

    45 minutes

1 basic recipe Victory Filling (Recipe 2)
3 tablespoons grated toasted almonds
3 eggs, beaten
24 whole almonds
fat for frying
    About 24 croquettes

Make very small croquettes of Victory Filling and coat them
with grated almonds. Dip in eggs and again in the grated almonds.
Stick a whole almond in center of each croquette and fry in deep
fat until golden brown, turning once. Serve hot.

7. Spicy Appetizers (Salgadinhos Picantes)

45 minutes

2 cups grated Parmesan cheese
½ cup sour cream
1 cup chopped ham
½ cup chopped olives
2 tablespoons chopped sour pickles
2 cups chopped toasted peanuts
24 round salted crackers
mustard
butter
24 canapés

Mix until creamy the first 5 ingredients, reserving a little of the cheese. Make small balls and coat them with the chopped peanuts. Spread each cracker thinly with mustard, place a cheese ball on each, finish with a dab of cheese and butter mixed together.

8. Dolphins (Dolphins)

45 minutes

1 onion, chopped
3 tablespoons oil
3 small tomatoes, peeled and chopped
1 dash black pepper
1 pound shrimp or 1 large can dry-pack shrimp
6 tablespoons tomato paste
1 cup milk
2 tablespoons rice flour
butter
24 slices toast
mayonnaise
24 canapés

Brown onion in oil and add tomatoes and black pepper. Cook for a few minutes and add shrimp, which have been cooked in a little water, shelled, and cleaned. Let cook for about 10 minutes over low flame and add tomato paste. Cook 5 minutes, then remove shrimp. Mix milk with rice flour; gradually add to the sauce, and cook until creamy. Butter 24 small molds. Place a shrimp in bottom of each mold, fill with the sauce, smooth top with knife, and chill. Spread each slice of toast with mayonnaise, loosen the sauce in the mold gently with a thin knife, and turn onto the toast.

9. STUFFED PRUNES (Ameixas Recheadas)

45 minutes

3 hard-cooked egg yolks
3 tablespoons butter
2 tablespoons grated toasted almonds
3 tablespoons chopped ham
1 teaspoon mustard
24 large prunes, pitted
24 small pieces ham
24 canapés

Mash egg yolks and butter into a smooth paste, add almonds, ham, and mustard. Stuff prunes with this mixture and stick a piece of ham in the center of each.

10. SHRIMP CANAPÉS (Canapés de Camarões)

35 minutes

6 slices toast, cut into quarters
24 slices hard-cooked eggs
24 small slices ham
24 prunes, pitted
24 shrimps, cooked and cleaned
mayonnaise
24 canapés

Place a slice of egg on each piece of toast. Cover with a slice of ham and a prune, which has been cut into star shape. Place a shrimp upright in the center of each, holding it with toothpick. Garnish with a dab of mayonnaise.

11. HAM AND ASPARAGUS CANAPÉS
(Canapés de Presunto e Aspargo)

20 minutes

12 rectangular slices rye bread
12 rectangular slices boiled ham
36 asparagus tips
12 slices smoked raw ham
6 black olives, pitted
mayonnaise
    12 canapés

Place slices of boiled ham on bread slices (about 1½ inches ×
2½ inches). Roll 3 asparagus tips in each slice of smoked raw
ham, place over boiled ham, garnish with half an olive and a small
amount of mayonnaise.

12. RYE BREAD AND CHEESE CANAPÉS
(Canapés de Pão de Centeio e Queijo)

½ hour

24 triangular pieces rye bread or pumpernickel
24 triangular slices Gruyère cheese
24 slices radish
water cress
mayonnaise
    24 canapés

Cut bread and cheese the same size and place cheese on bread.
Cut radish slices into flower shapes and place on cheese, and add
sprig of water cress with 2 small leaves. Trace a line of mayonnaise
around the edges of canapés over the cheese.

13. PIQUANT BANANAS (Bananas Picantes)

35 minutes
8 bananas
lemon juice
breast of 1 large roasted chicken
½ cup mayonnaise
16 canapés

Cut the bananas in half lengthwise and remove pulp very carefully. Cut pulp into small pieces and sprinkle with lemon juice. Sprinkle the shell of banana with lemon juice. Cut up the breast of chicken very fine, add banana pieces, and mayonnaise. Pile this mixture into the banana shells and garnish with a piece of the banana.

14. CAVIAR SHELLS (Barquetas de Caviar)

1 hour 45 minutes
5 tablespoons flour
2 tablespoons butter
1 dash salt
1 egg
uncooked rice
caviar
lemon juice
chives, finely chopped
lettuce
24 canapés

Mix flour, butter, salt, and egg until smooth and creamy. Let stand for 1 hour and roll out ⅛ inch thick on lightly floured board. Line small, oblong, greased baking shells with this dough. Prick bottom of each shell with fork and fill with uncooked rice. Bake about 15 minutes, or until golden brown. Take out rice, discard, and fill shells with caviar, sprinkle with a few drops of lemon juice and finely chopped chives. Serve on a crystal plate garnished with lettuce leaves.

These shells may be filled with any mixture, such as chicken or shrimp salad.

15. SWEETBREAD SHELLS (Barquetas Delicias)

50 minutes
1 sweetbread
1 tablespoon salt
1 teaspoon scraped onion
mayonnaise
1 dash pepper
chives, finely chopped
    About 12 canapés

Cook sweetbread in water and salt for about 25 minutes. Remove and plunge into cold water, remove membranes, and cut up fine with a knife. Add onion and enough mayonnaise to hold mixture together, fill the shells (Recipe 14), sprinkle with pepper and the chopped chives.

16. SALAD SHELLS (Barquetas de Ovos)

45 minutes
2 small freshly cooked potatoes, very finely chopped
2 tart apples, finely chopped
1 hard-cooked egg, chopped
1 raw carrot, grated
1 cucumber pickle, chopped
½ cup cooked, drained peas
¼ teaspoon salt
pepper
few drops Worcestershire sauce
few drops vinegar
mayonnaise
1 can sardines in oil
24 slices hard-cooked eggs
parsley, chopped
    About 24 canapés

Mix together the first 10 ingredients and let mixture stand for about ½ hour. Add enough mayonnaise to bind. Fill shells (Recipe 14) with this mixture. Decorate with strips of sardine and slices of egg; finish with chopped parsley.

17. CHEESE DELIGHTS (Bocados de Queijo)

    35 minutes

    8 tablespoons mashed cream cheese
    8 tablespoons grated Parmesan cheese
    2 tablespoons butter
    4 raw egg yolks
    ½ teaspoon salt
    1 dash nutmeg
    12 slices sandwich bread
      24 canapés

Cream first 6 ingredients together. Cut each slice of bread in half, remove crust, and toast on one side only. Spread a generous amount of cheese mixture cn toasted side of bread. Put on buttered baking sheet and bake for about 10 minutes. Serve hot.

18. CHEESE PUFFS (Delicias de Queijo)

    1 hour

    2 egg whites
    1 dash salt
    grated cheese
    1 cup dry bread crumbs
    oil for frying
    parsley, chopped
      About 24 canapés

Beat egg whites and salt until stiff and add enough cheese to handle as a dough. Make little balls the size of a walnut. Coat them with bread crumbs. Fry in hot oil and serve hot, sprinkled with chopped parsley.

19. CHURRASQUINHOS (*shur-ra-skee'-nyos*)

45 minutes
1 pound beef tenderloin
⅛ cup olive oil
2 tablespoons lemon juice
salt
pepper
1 tablespoon minced onion
½ pound sliced bacon
    24 *churrasquinhos*

Cut the beef tenderloin in slices, then in cubes (about ¾ inch square). Marinate in oil, lemon juice, salt, pepper, and minced onion for at least ½ hour, longer if convenient. Cut bacon in squares and put alternating bacon and beef squares on toothpicks until full. Put under grill and cook until brown. Serve very hot.

20. HAM MOLDS (Formas de Presunto)

1 hour
6 slices white bread
1 cup milk
1 small onion
butter
parsley, chopped
3 slices ham, chopped
2 tablespoons grated Parmesan cheese
1 dash salt
3 whole eggs
    About 24 canapés

Soak the bread slices in milk and put through sieve. Sauté onion in butter until golden brown and add parsley and bread. Cook for a few minutes. Add chopped ham and remove from heat. Add cheese and salt and fold in the 3 eggs, slightly beaten. Pour this mixture into small greased cupcake pans and bake in moderate oven for about 20 to 25 minutes, or until light brown. Pass a thin knife around each little cake and remove gently from pan. Serve hot.

21. DELICIOUS PAULISTA ROLLS (Enroladinhos Paulistas)

    1 hour 15 minutes
    ½ pound cream cheese
    ½ pound butter
    2 cups flour
    1 dash salt
    chopped ham
    24 frankfurter pieces, 1½ inches long
    1 egg yolk
    About 24 canapés

Mix cheese, butter, flour, and salt. Knead this dough well and let it stand for 1 hour. Roll out ⅛ inch thick and cut into 1½–2½-inch pieces. Sprinkle each piece with chopped ham. Roll up each with a piece of frankfurter and brush with egg yolk. Bake in moderate oven for about 15 minutes. Serve piping hot.

22. HAM DREAMS (Sonhos de Presunto)

    1 hour
    2 cups milk
    2 cups flour
    1 cup chopped ham
    2 tablespoons melted butter
    1 dash salt
    3 egg whites, well beaten
    oil for frying
    About 24 canapés

Mix the milk with the flour gradually to make a smooth paste, add chopped ham, melted butter, and salt. Put over low flame and cook, stirring constantly, until the flour has a clear, cooked appearance. Cool. Fold in the egg whites and drop by tablespoons in very hot oil. Fry until golden brown and serve hot.

23. SABARÁ APPETIZERS (Salgadinhos Sabará)

1 hour 15 minutes

½ onion, chopped
2 tablespoons butter
1 dash red pepper
3 tablespoons flour
2 cups milk
2 egg yolks
2 cups chopped ham
salt
1 cup grated Parmesan cheese
½ cup soft bread crumbs
olives, pitted
1 whole egg, slightly beaten
½ cup fine dry bread crumbs
oil for frying
    About 24 canapés

Sauté the onion in butter and add pepper and flour. Add the milk gradually, egg yolks, ham, and salt. Cook for 10 minutes. Remove from heat and add Parmesan cheese and soft bread crumbs. Mix well and make little balls the size of large marbles. Press a small piece of olive into the center of each ball, coat in the slightly beaten egg, roll in dry bread crumbs, and fry in deep hot oil. Serve hot.

24. PLAZA PRUNES (Ameixas Plaza)

1 hour 15 minutes

1 pound large prunes
1 cup toasted and ground peanuts
1½ cups mashed cream cheese
2 tablespoons mayonnaise
    About 50 prunes

Soak the prunes for about ½ hour. Drain, dry, and remove the pits very carefully. Mix peanuts with cream cheese and mayonnaise. Stuff prunes with this mixture and place each in a little, fancy paper cup to serve.

25. PICKLE AND RAISIN SANDWICH (Sanduiche de Pepino)

35 minutes
2 hard-cooked eggs
½ cup finely chopped sweet pickles
1 cup ground raisins
mayonnaise
1 loaf sandwich bread
butter
lettuce
24 sandwiches

Mash the eggs well, add pickles, raisins, and enough mayonnaise to moisten well. Cut the sandwich bread lengthwise in thin slices. Butter a slice of the bread lightly, spread with filling, cover with lettuce leaves and another layer of filling, and top with another slice of buttered bread. Cut into small oblong sandwiches, or into squares or triangles.

26. SOUTH AMERICAN SANDWICH (Sanduiche Sul-Americano)

½ hour
1 avocado, mashed smooth
½ cup chopped green olives
1 teaspoon scraped onion
1 dash red pepper
mayonnaise
salt
strips of pimento
6 slices white bread
24 small open-face sandwiches

Mix the avocado with olives, onion, red pepper, and enough mayonnaise to spread. Taste to see if salt is necessary. Spread on the 6 slices of bread (from which the crusts have been removed); cut each slice in 4 pieces. Decorate each with a strip of pimento.

27. SHRIMP SANDWICH (Sanduiche de Camarão)

45 minutes

1 small onion, chopped
4 tablespoons oil
1 pound fresh shrimp, cooked and cleaned, or 1 large can dry-pack
  shrimp
1 cup heavy cream, or enough to moisten shrimp
1 teaspoon salt
1 dash black pepper
½ teaspoon mustard
butter
12 slices sandwich bread
24 sandwiches

Cook the onion lightly in the oil, add the shrimp, and cook for
10 minutes if raw, or 1 minute if canned. Grind and add enough
heavy cream to make a smooth paste, add salt, pepper, and mustard. Make sandwiches of this mixture on lightly buttered bread;
cut in desired shapes.

28. TONGUE SANDWICH (Sanduiche de Lingua)

45 minutes

½ pound canned tongue
3 tablespoons flour
1 cup milk
1 egg yolk
2 tablespoons chopped pickle or pickle relish
butter
12 slices sandwich bread
mayonnaise
24 sandwiches

Grind the tongue. Mix flour, milk, and egg yolk and cook over
low flame, stirring constantly until thick. Add tongue and pickles.
Cool. Spread this mixture on each slice of buttered bread, cut in
halves, and spread with a layer of mayonnaise.

29. "Drumsticks" (Coxinhas de Galinha)

2½ hours

1 young chicken, 4 pounds
1 tablespoon chopped onion
2 tablespoons butter
6 cups water
1 sprig parsley
1 tablespoon salt
2 cups milk
12 tablespoons flour
4 egg yolks, well beaten
fine dry bread crumbs
3 eggs, beaten
fat for frying
15 "drumsticks"

Clean and cut up the chicken. Cook the onion lightly in the butter, add chicken, water, parsley and salt. Cover and cook slowly until tender. As chicken cooks, taste to see if there is enough salt. Remove chicken from broth, cool a little, and carefully remove skin and meat from the bones, being careful to keep the pieces whole, or as large as possible. Strain the broth (there should be about 2 cups); if very fat, skim off some of the fat, but some can be left. Mix enough of the cold milk into the flour to make smooth paste; mix this into the rest of the milk and the 2 cups of chicken broth. Stir over a low flame until it thickens. Put a few spoonfuls of this cream into the 4 egg yolks and mix well, then return to kettle and cook, stirring constantly, until the egg yolks have thickened the cream. It should be quite stiff, as for croquettes. Spread the fine bread crumbs on a board and put a large spoonful of this cream (still warm) on the crumbs and place on this a piece of chicken. Roll the chicken in the cream and the crumbs, forming a croquette. The larger pieces of chicken can be divided, so the pieces are of uniform size. Insert a piece of bone in each piece so that it resembles a drumstick. You can separate the wing bones to use, and if you run out of bones, you may break pieces of raw macaroni into proper lengths and use as bones. Dip "drumsticks" in beaten eggs, again in bread crumbs, and fry in hot deep fat until golden brown.

30. Puffy Cheese Empadinha *em-pa-deen'-ya*
(Empadinha de Queijo)

   1 hour 15 minutes
1¼ cups pastry flour
1 teaspoon salt
3 tablespoons butter
1 egg yolk
   18 small *empadinhas*

Sift pastry flour with salt, work into it the butter and egg yolk.
Press this pastry into small cupcake pans, and fill with the following:

2 cups grated American cheese
1 cup milk
1½ tablespoons melted butter
4 eggs, well beaten

Mix all the ingredients and pour into the pastry-lined pans. Bake
for about 25 minutes in a 350-degree oven, or until pastry and filling are golden brown.

Soups

Soup is almost always the first course of any dinner in Brazil. When the weather is very hot, a cold jellied Consommé (Recipe 32) may be served. Rich, dark brown Black Bean Soup (Recipe 37) garnished with sliced egg and croutons, served in your nicest bowls or cups, will brighten the eyes of your family or guests on a cold winter day. *Canja* (chicken soup; Recipe 33) is substantial enough to use for a luncheon or supper dish. Creamy, hot Artichoke-heart Soup (Recipe 34) will bring exclamations of delight from your dinner or luncheon guests.

31. STOCK FOR SOUP (Caldo de Carne)

5 hours

3 pounds soup meat
1 pound bones
6 quarts water
2 tablespoons salt
2 onions
4 cloves
6 carrots
3 turnips
1 bunch parsley
2 whole green onions
1 small bay leaf, or ½ large bay leaf
3 quarts

Put the meat and bones to cook with the water; when it boils, take off all the scum, add salt and all the remaining ingredients. Cover and simmer for about 4 hours, or until meat is perfectly tender. Let cool a little, skim off the fat, and strain.

32. CONSOMMÉ (Consomé)

3 hours

2 quarts stock (Recipe 31)
1 pound ground lean meat
1 leek, white part only
2 egg whites, beaten
lemon slices
chopped parsley (optional)
    6 servings

Put all the ingredients except egg whites in a kettle and cook for
1½ hours. Add egg whites. Let cool, remove any fat there may be
on top, strain through a napkin which has been moistened with
cold water. Taste for salt. Serve hot or ice-cold-jellied, in cups,
garnished with slice of lemon or chopped parsley. For a more
hearty consommé you may poach an egg to put into each cup.

33. BRAZILIAN CHICKEN SOUP (Canja à Brasileira)

4 hours

stewing chicken, 5 pounds
2 quarts water
2 teaspoons salt
½ cup rice
½ small onion, chopped
1 carrot, finely diced
1 small clove garlic, crushed
½ teaspoon pepper
1 small tomato, peeled, seeded, and chopped
1 teaspoon chopped parsley
1 teaspoon chives or chopped green onion
1 sprig mint, chopped
    6 servings

Disjoint the chicken and cook with water and salt for 2 hours,
or until tender. Add rice, onion, carrot, garlic, and pepper, and
cook until rice is well cooked and chicken is tender. Add finely
cut-up tomato when almost done, for color. Put in parsley, chives
or chopped green onion, and mint, and serve. Pieces of the chicken
may be served in the soup plate or separately.

34. ARTICHOKE-HEART SOUP (Sopa de Alcachofras)

45 minutes

10 artichoke hearts
1 small onion, chopped fine
8 cups water
2 teaspoons salt
2 cups rich milk
1 tablespoon corn meal
salt
2 tablespoons butter
6 tablespoons grated Parmesan cheese
½ cup croutons
6 servings

Cut up artichoke hearts, add onion, and cook in water and salt until tender. Mix a little of the cold milk with the corn meal and add to soup, with the rest of the milk. Cook until it thickens. Taste for salt. Add the butter and grated cheese. Serve and place a spoonful of the croutons on each plate.

35. ONION SOUP (Sopa de Cebolas)

1 hour

3 large onions
2 tablespoons butter
1 tablespoon flour
6 cups beef stock
1 tablespoon pepper
butter
6 slices lightly toasted French bread
1 cup grated Parmesan cheese
6 servings

Cut onions in very thin slices and brown lightly in butter, add flour and mix, add stock and pepper and cook for 10 minutes. Butter the toast slices and put in 6 individual ovenproof bowls. Fill bowls with stock mixture, sprinkle with the Parmesan cheese, bake for about 20 minutes in a 400-degree oven.

36. Vegetable Soup (Sopa de Legumes)

3 hours

1 pound lean soup meat
2 potatoes
3 carrots
1 large onion
3 stalks of celery
1 small sweet potato
1 2-inch-square piece of squash
1 tablespoon salt
1 tablespoon butter
4 servings

Boil meat and vegetables very slowly in enough water to cover well, until perfectly tender, adding the salt and, if necessary, a little water. Remove meat, put all the rest through sieve. Return to fire and heat well, adding butter. Test for seasoning. The meat may be served separately.

37. Black Bean Soup (Sopa de Feijão Preto)

1 hour

2 cups cooked or leftover black beans
3 cups meat stock (Recipe 31)
1 onion
1 bay leaf
3 strips bacon, finely minced
salt
1 or 2 tomatoes (optional)
1 hard-cooked egg, sliced
croutons
6 to 8 servings

Put beans, stock, and onion in the blender and grind until it is very fine. It should be of cream-soup consistency, but if not, add a little water. Put mixture in double boiler over boiling water, add the bay leaf and the bacon. Cook for about 45 minutes. Add salt to taste as it cooks—the quantity depends on whether the beans were freshly cooked or left over. You may make this soup with cooked navy beans, or even leftover baked beans, in which case add a tomato or two, to balance the sweet taste. Serve topped with slice of hard-cooked egg and croutons.

38. WINE SOUP FOR DESSERT (Sopa de Vinho)

25 minutes
1 quart white wine
1 cup sugar
6 egg yolks, beaten
6 to 8 servings

Mix all the ingredients and cook over a low flame, stirring constantly until foamy. Do not let boil. Serve hot with ladyfingers or your favorite cookies.

"*Peixeiro, siri, camarões! Quem quer comprar?*"—"Fish man! Crabs, shrimp! Who wants to buy?"—calls the fish vender. The fishing boats come in early in the morning with their haul, and even on the fashionable and famous Copacabana Beach, we see the fishermen bringing in their nets, and can buy a fish still alive and wriggling. Deep-sea fishing is a popular sport—and what could be more delightful for a fisherman than pulling in lots of fish under blue tropical skies. In the interior, the fishermen who fish the rivers can also tell you about "the big one that got away." But he must be careful, because of the *nêgo d'agua*, a dark hairy man who lives in the river, who will pull the canoe and its occupant under the water if he is in the mood—and if he does, they will never be seen again!

From Bahia comes the delicious Muqueca (Recipe 39), and in Rio de Janeiro you eat fillets of haddock with Shrimp Sauce (Recipe 40) and Fillet of Sole Veneziano, sole cooked in white wine, served on a bed of seasoned spinach, covered with Mornay Sauce (Recipe 58).

Salt codfish is prepared in a variety of interesting ways, especially during Lent and Holy Week, and a species of fresh codfish is used in the northern part of Brazil.

39. MUQUECA BAHIANA   (*moo-keh'-kah*)

   3 hours

3 onions
2 cloves garlic, minced (optional)
1½ teaspoons salt
juice of 2 lemons
6 fish fillets (halibut, lake trout)
4 tomatoes, peeled and chopped
2 green peppers, chopped
½ cup olive oil
1½ cups coconut milk
2 tablespoons *dendê*, corn, or peanut oil
1 cup hot water
salt
2 tablespoons flour
   6 servings

Chop 2 of the onions, mix with garlic, salt, and lemon juice, and marinate the fish in this for 2 hours. Put over flame in heavy pan. Add the tomatoes, the green peppers, the other onion, chopped, the olive oil, ¾ cup of the coconut milk, the *dendê* or other oil, and cook for 25 minutes, or until fish is tender. Lift the fish out carefully onto a hot platter and keep hot. Add the hot water and a little salt to the mixture in the pan, and put all through a sieve. Bring to a boil and add the rest of the coconut milk and thicken the sauce with the flour mixed with a little cold water. Pour sauce over fish fillets and serve at once.

40. Fish, Rio de Janeiro Style, with Shrimp Sauce (Peixe à Rio de Janeiro)

2 hours

4 pounds fillet of haddock or fresh codfish
1 onion, chopped
1 clove garlic, minced
1 teaspoon paprika
3½ teaspoons salt
2 tablespoons butter
1 tablespoon lard
½ cup flour
1 whole egg
4 tablespoons milk
1 egg yolk
6 pieces palm heart or artichoke heart
6 to 8 servings

Season fish with onion, garlic, paprika, and 3 teaspoons salt and cook for 20 minutes in enough water to cover. Remove from water, take off skin, and remove bones and break into large flakes. Save the water in which fish was cooked. Prepare a dough with the butter and lard worked into the flour, add ½ teaspoon salt, egg, and milk mixed together. Roll out to ¼ inch in thickness, and cut into oblongs, 1×4 inches. Cut off the corners of one end of each to make a point. Place on greased baking sheet, brush tops with egg yolk, and bake in 350-degree oven for about 20 minutes.

SHRIMP SAUCE

2 pounds prawns or shrimp
or
2 cans shrimp
2 onions, sliced
2 tomatoes, peeled and sliced
4 tablespoons butter
3 cups fish water
2 tablespoons flour
1 tablespoon tomato paste
½ teaspoon salt

Wash and shell and remove dark vein from prawns or shrimp. Fry onions and tomatoes in 2 tablespoons of the butter for about

10 minutes and put through sieve. Return to fire with the prawns or shrimp and the 3 cups of fish water. Cook 10 minutes, remove shrimp or prawns, and set aside (if shrimp are canned, cook only 5 minutes). Thicken the liquid with the flour and remaining butter, add tomato paste and salt, simmer until thick. Test for seasoning.

Place flakes of haddock in center of platter, surrounded with palm or artichoke hearts. Pour sauce over this, and decorate with pastry points and prawns or shrimp.

41. ZORÔ (Zorô)

When you want something different and interesting, try this dish from North Brazil.

 1 hour 15 minutes
 ½ pound dried codfish
 ½ pound dried shrimp, cleaned
 2 tablespoons olive oil
 2 tablespoons butter
 2 onions, chopped
 1 summer squash or zucchini
 1 pound fresh shrimp, cleaned
 1 clove garlic, minced
 pepper
 ½ teaspoon salt
 ¾ cup coconut milk
 8 okra
 3 tablespoons *dendê*, corn, or peanut oil
  6 to 8 servings

Cook the codfish in small amount of water for 25 minutes, drain, remove skin and bones, and cut up. Cook dried shrimp for 10 minutes and grind. Make a *refogado* of the oil, butter, and 1 onion. Cut up squash and cook for 5 minutes in a small amount of water. Drain and add to the *refogado*. Add cooked codfish, dried shrimp, fresh shrimp, the other onion, the garlic, pepper, salt, and coconut milk. Cook for 20 minutes over low flame, add chopped okra and oil, and cook for 10 minutes longer. Serve hot with Fluffy Rice (Recipe 137).

42. CODFISH MOLDS (Forminhas de Bacalhau)

1½ hours

2 pounds dried codfish
1 tablespoon vinegar
1 tablespoon butter
12 green olives
8 cups hot cooked Fluffy Rice (Recipe 137)
3 cups hot, finely chopped, drained spinach
spinach juice
12 molds

In plenty of water, cook the codfish with the vinegar for 25 minutes. Drain, skin, remove bones, and shred. Fry in 1 tablespoon butter. Put olive in the bottom of 12 individual molds, a layer of codfish, layer of rice, and layer of spinach. Put a spoonful of the spinach juice on top of each mold. Put molds in pan of hot water to keep hot, for 10 minutes. Unmold on hot platter and serve with following sauce:

SAUCE

1 cup milk
4 egg yolks, beaten
¼ cup tomato sauce
1 pound cooked shrimp
½ tablespoon chopped parsley
½ tablespoon chopped chives
salt

Make a custard of the milk and beaten egg yolks in the top of double boiler, keeping the water barely boiling and stirring constantly. Add tomato sauce, shrimp, parsley, and chives. Taste for salt. Cook for 5 minutes. This sauce may be served with any boiled or baked fish.

43. Codfish Muqueca *moo-keh'-kah* (Muqueca de Bacalhau)

1 hour

1 pound dried codfish
½ cup olive oil or other salad oil
3 small onions, chopped
3 small tomatoes, peeled and chopped
2 large green peppers, chopped
½ tablespoon chopped parsley
½ tablespoon chopped chives
1 dash hot pepper sauce
¼ cup *dendé*, corn, or peanut oil
3 tablespoons rice flour
1½ cups coconut milk
salt
4 to 6 servings

Soak the dried codfish in water overnight. Next day, remove skin and bones and cut into small pieces. Make a *refogado* of oil, onions, tomatoes, green peppers, parsley, chives, and pepper sauce. Add codfish and cook for 35 minutes over low heat, adding small amount of hot water if too dry. Add oil. Make a cream sauce of the rice flour mixed into the coconut milk with a little salt. Serve in a separate bowl as accompaniment to the codfish.

44. Dried Codfish, Paulista Style (Bacalhau Paulista)

1 hour 45 minutes

1 pound dried codfish
2 tablespoons flour
1 onion, chopped
½ tablespoon chopped parsley
3 tablespoons olive oil
2 cups milk
4 to 6 servings

Soak codfish in water overnight, drain, remove skin and bones, and cut in 2-inch squares. Dip squares in flour and set aside to dry. Fry onion and parsley in oil and remove from oil. Sauté codfish

in the same oil until golden brown. Place codfish, cooked onion
and parsley, and milk in a saucepan and cook over low flame for
about 1 hour, or until milk is absorbed. Serve hot.

45. PAULISTA OMELET (Fritada Paulista)

If you like codfish and want something unusual, try this, next fish
day.

> 1½ hours
> ½ pound dried codfish
> 3 tablespoons oil
> 1 small onion, chopped
> ½ tablespoon chopped parsley
> 1 dash cayenne pepper
> 1 cup milk
> ¾ cup coconut milk
> 1 cup mashed potatoes
> 3 egg yolks, beaten
> 3 whole eggs
> ¼ teaspoon salt
> 6 servings

Soak the dried codfish in water overnight, then remove skin and
bones, and shred. Make a *refogado* with oil, onion, parsley, and
pepper, add codfish and fry lightly for a few minutes, then cover
with milk and coconut milk and cook until liquid is reduced by
one half. Add the potatoes and beaten egg yolks, stir, and cook
until thick. Add salt if necessary. Put mixture in greased casserole
and pour over it the whole eggs beaten with ¼ teaspoon salt. Bake
in a hot oven (375 degrees) for 10 or 15 minutes or until brown.

46. DRIED CODFISH IN BUTTER SAUCE
(Bacalhau com Môlho)

1 hour 15 minutes

1 pound dried codfish
1 onion, chopped
½ tablespoon chopped parsley
1 peeled and chopped lemon
3 tablespoons olive oil
¼ pound butter
1 pinch salt
1 dash pepper
6 slices bread
6 anchovies
  6 servings

Soak codfish overnight. Cook 25 minutes, remove skin and bones, and cut into 6 pieces. Cook the onion, parsley, and lemon in oil and butter. Add salt and pepper. Toast the bread. Place a piece of the codfish on each slice of bread, cover with sauce, and garnish with an anchovy.

47. CODFISH BALLS, BRAZILIAN STYLE
(Bolinhos de Bacalhau)

1 hour 15 minutes

½ pound dried codfish
1 tablespoon butter
1 small onion, chopped
½ tablespoon chopped chives
½ tablespoon chopped parsley
1 cup milk
5 medium-sized potatoes, cooked and mashed
3 tablespoons flour
4 eggs
½ teaspoon paprika
salt
oil for frying
  6 to 8 servings

Soak codfish overnight. Cook 25 minutes and remove skin and bones. Chop. Make a *refogado* with butter, onion, chives, and parsley. Mix with codfish and add milk, potatoes, flour, eggs and paprika, and salt if necessary. Drop by tablespoons into hot oil and fry until golden brown. Serve hot.

48. Sole Fillets with Pineapple (Fatias de Peixe com Abacaxi)

You may use your favorite fish for this recipe. It is equally delicious with salt or fresh-water fish.

1 hour 15 minutes
6 fillets of sole or other fish
1 teaspoon salt
juice of 1 lemon
1 cup milk
3 tablespoons flour
½ cup oil
6 slices fresh or canned pineapple
3 tablespoons butter
6 large potatoes, peeled
chopped parsley
melted butter
6 servings

Season fish with salt and lemon juice and dip in the milk and flour, which has been mixed. Sauté in oil until golden brown. Sauté pineapple slices in butter. Have the potatoes boiling in salted water. When cooked, pile them in the center of a hot platter, sprinkle with parsley, and pour on melted butter. Surround with pineapple slices, and place a fish fillet on each slice of pineapple, and serve very hot.

49. MARINATED FISH (Peixe à Escabeche)

For this dish, you may use any fish that will cut into firm slices.

3 hours
1 fish, about 2 pounds
1 tablespoon salt
1 clove garlic, minced
1 teaspoon pepper
juice of 1 lemon
1 cup oil
3 onions, sliced
6 small tomatoes, peeled and finely chopped
½ cup vinegar
6 to 8 servings

Cut the cleaned fish into slices, season with salt, ½ clove garlic, pepper, and lemon juice. Soak for 2 hours; then drain and fry in the oil, reserving 4 tablespoons of the oil for sauce. In a separate pan, cook the onions, the tomatoes, the other ½ clove garlic, and vinegar with 4 tablespoons oil. Bring to a boil and let simmer for a few minutes. Remove from flame. Place a layer of fish and a layer of sauce alternately in a deep dish. Let stand until next day in refrigerator, and serve cold.

50. BAHIA BAKED FISH WITH TOMATO SAUCE (Peixe Assado à Baiana)

3 hours
2 1½-pound fishes, cleaned
juice of 3 lemons
1 tablespoon salt
½ clove garlic, minced
½ tablespoon chopped parsley
1 onion, chopped
⅓ pound manioc flour, or fine, dry bread crumbs
3 tablespoons butter
½ pound prunes, pitted
2 hard-cooked eggs, chopped
½ pound fresh or canned shrimp, cleaned
6 to 8 servings

Remove spine and bones of 1 fish, being careful to keep the fish whole. Marinate in lemon juice, salt, garlic, parsley, and onion for at least ½ hour. Turn occasionally.

Cook the other fish in a little water and salt. Brown the manioc flour or bread crumbs in butter, add the prunes, more salt, chopped eggs, whole shrimp, and chopped boned cooked fish. Mix well. Stuff the marinated fish with this mixture, and bake in a 400-degree oven for about ½ hour. Shake occasionally to prevent sticking. Serve with Tomato Sauce, below:

TOMATO SAUCE

    1 onion, chopped
    1 carrot, cut in thin slices
    4 tablespoons butter
    parsley, chopped
    ½ bay leaf
    3 tablespoons flour
    2 cups fresh or canned tomatoes, peeled and cut up
    1 teaspoon sugar
    1 teaspoon salt
    1 dash pepper

Cook the onion and carrot in 2 tablespoons butter, add parsley, bay leaf, and flour. Mash up the tomatoes and mix with the onion and carrot mixture, add sugar, salt, and pepper. Cover the pan and put it into a moderate oven for 45 minutes, stirring now and then so it will not burn. Press the mixture through a fine sieve and add the other 2 tablespoons of butter. Reheat to serve with the baked fish.

51. FISH PUDDING (Pudim de Peixe)

    1½ hours
    1 1-pound fish
    3 slices day-old white bread
    ½ cup milk
    6 egg yolks, beaten
    ½ tablespoon chopped parsley
    2 tablespoons melted butter
    ½ teaspoon salt
    3 egg whites, beaten
      6 to 8 servings

Cook the fish in enough salted water to cover. Remove from flame, take out spine and bones, and return to water. Cook until dry. Press through a sieve, or mash very fine. Remove crusts from bread, soak in milk, press through a sieve, add fish purée, beaten egg yolks, parsley, melted butter, and salt. Taste for. salt. Fold in beaten whites and cook in top of double boiler over boiling water for 15 minutes. Then turn it into a buttered baking dish and bake for ½ hour at 400 degrees.

52. SARDINE PUDDING (Pudim de Sardinhas)

   1 hour 25 minutes
   5 large potatoes, mashed
   1 large can sardines
   1 cup oil
   1 large onion, chopped
   ½ tablespoon chopped parsley
   1 teaspoon salt
   ½ teaspoon pepper
   6 eggs, well beaten
   butter
   bread crumbs
   mayonnaise
   lettuce, shredded
   2 hard-cooked eggs, sliced
   carrot strips, raw or cooked
   green peas, cooked
      8 servings

Mix mashed potatoes and sardines (free of bones and skin). Make a *refogado* of the oil, onion, parsley, salt, and pepper. Remove from flame and add to sardines and potatoes. Mix well, add eggs. Turn into buttered pan lined with bread crumbs and bake in oven at 400 degrees for 20 minutes, or until the mixture shrinks away from the sides of the pan. Store it in the refrigerator until cool. To serve, remove from pan, decorate with mayonnaise, and garnish with finely shredded lettuce, hard-cooked-egg slices, cooked or raw carrot strips, green peas, etc.

53. CRAB MEAT WITH SHERRY (Pudim de Siri)

1 hour

2 cups fresh crab meat
salt
1 dash pepper
1 level tablespoon corn meal
½ cup rich milk
2 tablespoons butter
¼ cup sherry wine
6 servings

Cook the crab meat in a little water with salt and pepper. Mix the corn meal with the milk and cook in double boiler until thick, add crab meat and the water in which it was cooked. Add the butter. Taste for salt. Remove from flame and add sherry. Serve hot over rice or in patty shells.

54. STUFFED CRABS (Siri Recheado)

45 minutes

2 tablespoons butter
1 tablespoon flour
⅔ cup water
2 egg yolks, beaten
salt
1 dash pepper
2 tablespoons white wine
2 cups cooked crab meat
1 tablespoon chopped parsley
2 tablespoons butter
½ cup dry bread crumbs
6 servings

Melt butter, add flour, mix well. Add water, cook until thick, remove from flame, and add beaten egg yolks. Return to flame, add salt, pepper, wine, and crab meat, and cook for a few minutes until thick. Add parsley and cool. Fill crab shells or individual Pyrex molds. Melt butter and rub into bread crumbs. Sprinkle crab meat with buttered crumbs and brown in hot oven (425 degrees) for about 10 minutes. Serve hot.

55. CRAB SPREAD FOR SANDWICHES (Manteiga de Siri para Sanduiches)

1½ hours

2 large-type crabs
6 small-type crabs
½ teaspoon salt
2 tablespoons butter
2 cups water
12 large sandwiches

Cook the crabs in salted boiling water for 5 minutes. Remove the meat from shells. On a board, pound the shells with butter and then boil with 2 cups water. Strain and cool in refrigerator. When cold, carefully remove the butter that has hardened on surface and mix with crab meat. This makes a delicious sandwich spread.

56. FAROFA (far-off'-ah) to serve with fish

15 minutes

1 pound manioc flour or fine dry bread crumbs
4 tablespoons butter
4 hard-cooked eggs
6 servings

Brown the manioc flour or the bread crumbs in a frying pan, stirring all the time. Add the butter—enough to moisten the manioc flour or crumbs well, but they should still remain loose and dry. Add the egg yolks, finely chopped. Pile on hot dish or platter and center with chopped whites. This is delicious with fish or with steaks or *churrasco* (barbecue).

57. CLAMS WITH RICE (Mariscos com Arroz)

    1 hour 15 minutes

24 clams
1 teaspoon salt
juice of 1 lemon
1 recipe Fluffy Rice (Recipe 137)
3 hard-cooked eggs, chopped
    6 servings

Put clams in hot water to facilitate opening of shells. Remove meat from shells and season with salt and lemon juice. Follow the recipe for Fluffy Rice, and shortly before the rice is cooked, add the clam meat, mix well, and finish cooking. Add chopped eggs just before serving.

58. FILLET OF SOLE VENEZIANO (Linguado Veneziano)

    1 hour 15 minutes

6 fillets of sole
1 cup white wine
1 pound or 1 can spinach
1 teaspoon salt
4 tablespoons butter
Mornay Sauce
2 cups grated cheese
    6 servings

Put the fillets in a pan and pour the wine over them. Cook very gently until fish is cooked, about 15 minutes. Cook the spinach in a small amount of salted water for 10 minutes, drain, and put on a board and chop with a knife until fine, then put it into a pan in which the butter has been melted and toss over the heat for a minute. Spread the spinach on a hot ovenproof platter, arrange the fish fillets on top, and cover with Mornay Sauce (below) and the cheese. Put in hot oven for 15 minutes, or until the cheese is brown.

3 tablespoons butter
3 tablespoons flour
2 cups milk
½ teaspoon salt
1 dash pepper
5 tablespoons grated Parmesan cheese

Melt butter, add flour, mix well, add milk, salt, and pepper and cook until thick. Add the grated cheese and pour over fish and spinach.

59. BAKED TROUT WITH WHITE WINE (Pescada ao Fôrno)

1 hour

2 trout about 2 pounds each, or other whole fish
2 teaspoons salt
juice of 1 lemon
1 clove garlic, finely minced
1 cup white wine
2 tablespoons chopped parsley
2 tablespoons chopped green onion
dry bread crumbs
4 tablespoons melted butter
6 servings

Clean the fish, leave them whole, cut two diagonal gashes on both sides of each. Rub with salt and lemon and marinate for 2 hours. Grease a baking dish well; sprinkle the minced garlic on the bottom of the pan. Lay the 2 fish on the garlic, sprinkle with the white wine and the parsley and onion, cover well with the bread crumbs, and spoon the melted butter over all. Bake for 25 to 30 minutes in a 400-degree oven. Serve in the baking dish.

60. Stuffed Fillets of Fish (Filés de Peixe Recheado)

> 1 hour

8 to 10 fish fillets
juice of 1 lemon
1 tablespoon salt
1 cup of fresh bread crumbs
4 eggs
2 tablespoons melted butter
2 tablespoons grated cheese
½ cup milk
2 cups of dry bread crumbs
oil for frying
lettuce
> 8 servings

Sprinkle fish with lemon and salt. Mix the fresh bread crumbs, 2 beaten eggs, melted butter, cheese, and milk. Put a spoonful on each fillet (cut in two if fillets are large), roll up, and fasten with toothpicks. Roll the fillets in crumbs, 2 beaten eggs, and crumbs, and fry in hot oil. Serve garnished with lettuce leaves.

61. Fish Fillets with Oysters and Wine (Filés de Peixe com Ostras)

> 1 hour

8 to 10 fish fillets
2 tablespoons salt
1 dash pepper
1½ cups white wine
2 tablespoons finely minced onion
½ cup olive oil
6 small tomatoes, peeled and cut in pieces
24 fresh oysters (small)
1 teaspoon lemon juice
2 teaspoons butter
flour
oil for sautéing
> 8 servings

Season the fish fillets with salt and pepper and let soak in wine for 2 hours. Brown the onion in the oil, add tomatoes, cook for 10 or 15 minutes, or until tomatoes are thoroughly cooked. Add the oysters, lemon, and butter, and boil gently for 10 minutes. Dip the fillets in flour, let dry a few minutes, sauté in the hot oil, and serve on a hot platter with oyster sauce.

SHRIMP

Brazil is a paradise for shrimp lovers, because we have hundreds of delicious dishes made of that succulent shellfish. Here are the recipes for the best and most traditional. You will find peculiar names of Indian and African origin (Vatapá, Acarajé, Caruru, and Efó), for which there is no translation, so I leave the names as they are and shall try to indicate pronunciation for you. The recipes may seem strange, but do not be afraid to try them, as they are considered delicious by foreigners as well as Brazilians.

Conventional shrimp recipes are included along with the more exotic ones. Breaded Shrimp Milanese (Recipe 76), Bahia Shrimp Pudding (Recipe 74), and Brazilian Empadinhas (Recipe 81) are good examples of what Brazilians can do with shrimp. From the state of Maranhão comes the Shrimp "Pie" (Recipe 84), which is described as a dish that puts "*água na boca*" ("water in the mouth"). This is almost a glorified omelet, but whatever it may be, it is worth the time you put into its preparation.

Fresh shrimp is of course the sweetest and finest-flavored, but frozen shrimp is a good substitute, except where the recipe calls for heads and shells to make a broth. You should remember that any shrimp recipe is improved if you have this rich shrimp broth available to use instead of water, even in your own favorite shrimp recipe. If you use powdered milk with the broth instead of the milk which the recipe sometimes calls for, the results will be— well, try it, and see for yourself.

62. VATAPÁ (vah-tah-pah')

Famous throughout the world, Vatapá is a traditional Afro-Brazilian dish. It is made of fish, shellfish, or sometimes meat, with manioc flour, *dendê* oil, and hot pepper. Here is the recipe made with shrimp, and adapted to the materials that you will be able to obtain.

> 1½ hours for Vatapá; 25 minutes for accompanying mold
> 6 slices white bread
> 1¾ cups coconut milk (thick)
> 1 onion, finely chopped
> 1 clove garlic, minced
> 1 teaspoon paprika
> ½ teaspoon cayenne pepper (optional)
> 1 teaspoon salt
> ½ teaspoon powdered ginger
> 2 pounds dried shrimp, or equal quantity canned or frozen shrimp, dried in the oven
> 1 cup toasted, finely chopped peanuts
> ⅔ cup finely chopped cashew nuts
> ¾ cup *dendê*, peanut, or corn oil
> 6 to 8 servings

Remove crusts from the bread and pour ¾ cup of the coconut milk over soft part and leave until it becomes soft. Then mash very fine, and add the onion, garlic, paprika, pepper, salt, and ginger, and mix very well. Shell the shrimp and pound or grind (it should be a fine mass). Add this to bread mixture along with the nuts. Add remaining coconut milk. Put over flame in heavy saucepan and cook, stirring constantly in same direction. Keep the flame low. Cook until thick. Add salt if it seems necessary. Mix in the oil and remove from flame. Serve with following mold, which you will have made early enough to have chilled thoroughly:

2 cups milk
¾ cup coconut milk
6 tablespoons rice flour
1 teaspoon salt
1 teaspoon pepper
1 tablespoon corn or peanut oil
butter

Mix the milk, coconut milk, rice flour, salt, and pepper and put over flame in heavy saucepan. Add the oil. Cook until thick, stirring constantly. Pour in a buttered mold and chill in the refrigerator. Unmold and serve very cold, in contrast to the Vatapá, which should be very hot.

63. Mock Vatapá   (Falso Vatapá)

45 minutes

2 pounds fresh shrimp, cleaned
2 tablespoons butter or margarine
1 pound dried shrimp, shelled
2 tablespoons peanut butter
3 tablespoons farina or white flour
1 cup warm water
1 tablespoon tomato paste
3 tablespoons *dendê*, peanut, or corn oil
1 teaspoon salt
½ teaspoon cayenne pepper (optional)
6 to 8 servings

Sauté the fresh shrimp in the butter or margarine. Cook the shelled dried shrimp 20 minutes and grind. Mix with peanut butter. Mix the farina or flour into the warm water and put over flame. Cook until it is quite thick, stirring all the time. Add tomato paste and oil. The mixture should be more or less as thick as mashed potatoes. Mix in all fresh and ground dried shrimp and heat well. Add salt if necessary (since the dried shrimps are rather salty, it is difficult to give exact quantity). Add pepper. Serve very hot in individual bowls.

64. Carurú à Bahiana ka-rew-rew' (Carurú Baiano)

Another dish of Sudanese origin, which is hot and spicy. You may use fewer or no peppers, it will still taste good.

> 1½ hours
> 1 pound okra
> 3 cups water
> 1 onion, chopped
> 1 teaspoon paprika
> 1 teaspoon salt
> 2 pounds dried shrimp, shelled
> 1 cup crushed cashew nuts
> 1 cup manioc flour or farina
> ½ cup peanut butter
> 3 tablespoons *dendê*, corn, or peanut oil
> 3 small dried hot peppers
> ½ teaspoon ginger
> 6 to 8 servings

Wash okra, cut off heads, and cut in small pieces. Put in a saucepan with 3 cups water, add onion, paprika, and salt. Cook until okra is tender. Put shrimp through grinder, or pound until it is a fine mass. Mix very well with cashew nuts and manioc flour or farina. Add peanut butter and just enough cold water to make a paste. Add this to the cooked okra while still boiling and stir constantly with a wooden spoon for 10 minutes. Add oil, peppers, and ginger. Serve hot, warm, or even cold, if you like.

65. Acarajé (a-cah-rah-jay')

Navy beans and shrimp made into a batter and fried crisp and brown. Very unusual and very delicious.

> 1 hour 15 minutes
> 2 cups navy beans
> 1 onion
> 2 cups fresh shrimp, cleaned
> 1 teaspoon salt
> 1 teaspoon pepper
> oil for frying
> 6 servings

Soak beans overnight, and the next day boil in salted water for 15 minutes, or until swollen and plump, and then grind with the onion and shrimp. Add salt and pepper and beat by hand or with rotary beater, or put in blender. The mixture should be very smooth. Drop by tablespoonfuls in hot oil and fry until golden brown. Remove from oil and drain on absorbent paper. Serve hot with Acarajé Sauce (Recipe 66).

66. ACARAJÉ SAUCE (Môlho de Acarajé)

½ hour

6 shrimps, cooked and minced
1 small onion, finely minced
4 small hot peppers
½ teaspoon salt
2 tablespoons *dendê*, corn, or peanut oil
6 servings

Mash shrimp, onion, and peppers together. Add salt. Use mortar and pestle if you have one. Add oil and cook for 10 minutes, stirring constantly.

67. EFÓ

1 hour

3 cups cooked spinach
1 pound dried shrimp, shelled
¾ cup coconut milk
6 tablespoons *dendê*, corn, or peanut oil
1 onion, minced
1 clove garlic, minced
1 teaspoon salt
6 servings

Press spinach through sieve and beat until smooth. Grind shrimp very fine, add coconut milk, oil, onion, garlic, and salt. Mix with spinach. Put in heavy saucepan and cook for 10 minutes, stirring constantly with wooden spoon, until mixture has the consistency of a pudding. Serve hot.

68. BAHIAN QUITUTE *key-too'-ty* (Quitute Baiano)

Quitute is the word for a tasty delicacy, and that is exactly what you would call this mixture of shrimp, coconut milk, and peanut butter served with a rice-flour mold.

1½ hours

2 tablespoons rice flour
¾ cup coconut milk
butter
1 pound dried shrimp, cleaned
6 tablespoons flour
2 cups milk
2 tablespoons peanut butter
2 tablespoons *dendê*, corn, or peanut oil
salt
　6 servings

Mix rice flour with coconut milk and cook until thick. Pour into buttered mold and chill. Cook the shrimp in a little water, grind, and set aside. Make a paste of the flour and milk and cook until thick, stirring constantly with a wooden spoon. Add shrimp and peanut butter, keep on cooking, and add oil little by little. Taste for salt. Unmold the rice-flour pudding and turn this mixture over it.

69. SHRIMP MOLDS FROM BAHIA (Camarão Baiano)

A delicious shrimp mixture baked and served in individual molds. This makes a nice luncheon dish.

> 1 hour 15 minutes
> ¼ cup *dendê*, peanut, or corn oil
> 1 large onion, chopped
> ½ tablespoon salt
> 2 green peppers, chopped
> 4 small tomatoes, peeled and chopped
> 2 pounds fresh shrimp, cleaned
> 1½ cups coconut milk
> corn meal
> butter
> 4 to 6 servings

Make a *refogado* of the oil, onion, salt, peppers, and tomatoes, and add the shrimp. Cook for about 15 minutes, add coconut milk, and continue cooking as you sift in a little corn meal—enough to give a thick, creamy consistency. Stir constantly while cooking. Pour into individual buttered molds, put them in a pan with 1 inch of hot water, and bake for ½ hour in a hot oven (400 degrees). Serve hot in mold.

70. SHRIMP MOLDS WITH CHEESE (Camarão com Queijo)

> 1 hour 15 minutes
> 2 pounds fresh shrimp, cleaned
> 2 tablespoons butter
> 2 tablespoons corn meal
> 1½ teaspoons salt
> 2 cups milk
> 1 cup plus 3 tablespoons grated Parmesan cheese
> butter
> 4 egg whites, beaten
> bread crumbs
> 6 to 8 servings

Chop the shrimp. Mix butter and corn meal, add 1 teaspoon salt, milk, and 1 cup cheese, and cook in saucepan until thick. Remove from flame, add shrimp, return to flame, and cook for 15 minutes. Turn into buttered mold and cover with the egg whites beaten stiff with ½ teaspoon salt. Sprinkle with rest of cheese and bread crumbs and bake until brown, or about 15 minutes, in a 400-degree oven.

71. SHRIMP PUDDING (Pudim de Camarão)

1½ hours

- 1 pound fresh shrimp, cleaned
- 2 teaspoons butter
- 2 tablespoons oil
- 3 eggs, beaten
- 1 cup mashed potatoes
- 1 teaspoon salt
- 3 tablespoons grated Parmesan cheese
- 2 tablespoons cornstarch
- 1 cup milk

bread crumbs

6 servings

Sauté shrimp in butter and oil until brown. Combine beaten eggs, mashed potatoes, salt, cheese, cornstarch, and milk, and mix in the shrimp. Turn into buttered casserole which has been dredged with bread crumbs, bake in 350-degree oven for 25 minutes, or until puffed and brown.

72. Shrimp Pie with Mashed-potato Crust (Torta de Camarão)

1½ hours

3 large potatoes, cooked and mashed
2 tablespoons flour
3 egg yolks
4 tablespoons grated Parmesan cheese
1 teaspoon salt
1 pinch nutmeg
½ pound fresh shrimp, cleaned
4 tablespoons oil
4 or 5 artichoke hearts, sliced
10 pitted olives, chopped
2 hard-cooked eggs, sliced
1 teaspoon capers
4 to 6 servings

Mix mashed potatoes, flour, 2 egg yolks, grated cheese, salt, and nutmeg. Line a large pie plate with about ⅔ of this mixture, leaving the rest for top crust. Fry the shrimp in the oil and arrange on bottom crust, next, the artichoke hearts, olives, egg slices, and capers, cover with remaining dough, smoothing it with a knife. Brush with the third egg yolk and bake in a 400-degree oven for 20 to 25 minutes. The egg yolk on crust gives a nice shiny yellow glaze. Serve hot.

73. BRAZILIAN SHRIMP (Camarão à Brasileira)

If you have fresh shrimp available, try this delicious dish, which is unusually rich in shrimp flavor because of the broth made with shrimp shells.

    1½ hours
2 pounds fresh shrimp
3 cups water
3 tablespoons butter
1 small onion, chopped
½ clove garlic, minced (optional)
1 tablespoon chopped parsley
1 large tomato, peeled and chopped
1 teaspoon salt
1 green pepper, chopped
3 egg yolks, beaten
3 tablespoons grated cheese
    6 servings

Remove the heads and shells from the shrimp, cook in the 3 cups water for 20 minutes, strain, reserving broth, and cook the shrimp in this broth for 10 minutes. Grind the shrimp. Make a *refogado* of the butter, onion, garlic, parsley, tomato, salt, and green pepper. Add to the shrimp water, along with the ground shrimp, and stir in the beaten egg yolks and grated cheese. Taste for salt. Serve this around a mound of Fluffy Rice (Recipe 137).

74. Delicious Bahia Shrimp Pudding
(Creme de Camarão)

2 hours

2 cups milk
6 tablespoons rice flour
1½ cups or 2 cans coconut milk
1 teaspoon salt
2 tablespoons olive oil
½ cup oil
1 onion, chopped
garlic powder or 2 cloves garlic (optional)
1 dash pepper
3 green peppers, chopped
1 pound tomatoes, peeled and chopped
1 teaspoon salt
1 pound large fresh shrimp, cleaned
1 bay leaf
1 teaspoon corn meal
3 tablespoons *dendê*, peanut, or corn oil
2 cups cooked spinach
  8 servings

Make a pudding of the milk, rice flour, ¾ cup coconut milk, salt, and 1 tablespoon of the olive oil. Pour into greased mold and chill. Make a *refogado* with the ½ cup oil and onion, garlic powder or 1 clove garlic, minced, pepper, chopped green peppers, cut-up tomatoes, and salt. Add shrimp and bay leaf and cook 15 minutes. Pour in ¾ cup coconut milk and cook for 10 minutes. Remove shrimp from sauce and strain the sauce. Thicken the sauce with the corn meal, remove from flame, and add *dendê* oil. Thoroughly drain the cooked spinach, and chop very fine, and put it into a pan with the second tablespoon of olive oil in which has been fried the other clove garlic, minced, or garlic powder.

Unmold the rice-flour pudding on a large platter, surround with the hot spinach, arrange shrimp over the pudding, and cover with sauce.

75. ARACY'S GOOD SHRIMP MAYONNAISE
(Camarão á Aracy com Maionese)

45 minutes

3 tablespoons olive oil
1 onion, chopped
1 tablespoon chopped parsley
1 teaspoon salt
1 dash pepper
1 pound fresh shrimp, cleaned
2 cups water
4 tablespoons cornstarch
butter
mayonnaise
pickles
4 to 6 servings

Make a *refogado* of oil, onion, ½ tablespoon parsley, salt, and pepper. Add shrimp and fry for a few minutes. Add water and cook for 10 minutes. Remove shrimp, save 4, and grind the rest. Return the ground shrimp to liquid and thicken with cornstarch. Pour into buttered mold and chill. Turn on a platter, garnish with the whole shrimps, chopped parsley, mayonnaise, and pickles.

76. SPECIAL BREADED SHRIMP MILANESE
(Camarões à Milanesa)

1½ hours

12 large shrimps, cleaned
juice of 2 lemons
1 tablespoon salt
6 servings

Soak the shrimps in lemon juice and salt for ½ hour. Stick a toothpick in each one and dip in clean water. Make the following coating:

¼ cup oil
2 tablespoons butter
1 tablespoon chopped chives or green-onion tops
2 tablespoons chopped parsley
1 tablespoon tomato paste
1 tablespoon finely chopped onion
½ pound small shrimp, cleaned and ground
6 slices day-old bread
1 cup milk
4 tablespoons flour
2 egg yolks
2 cups dry bread crumbs
oil for frying
lettuce

Make a *refogado* of oil and butter, chopped chives or green onion, parsley, tomato paste, and onion. Add the ground shrimp to the *refogado*. Have the bread soaked in the milk, mash it, and put it on to cook, stirring until it is smooth. Add this to the *refogado*, mix in the flour, and remove from heat. Cover each shrimp with this mixture, dip in egg yolks, roll in bread crumbs, and fry until brown in deep fat. Serve on a large platter decorated with lettuce leaves.

77. DELICIOUS SHRIMP   (Camarões Deliciosos)

45 minutes
1 pound fresh shrimp, cleaned
3 tablespoons butter
1 small onion, sliced
3 cups milk
4 tablespoons cornstarch
3 eggs
1 teaspoon salt
2 tablespoons grated Parmesan cheese
2 tablespoons dry bread crumbs
4 to 6 servings

Put the shrimp in a saucepan with 2 tablespoons butter and the onion and cook for 10 minutes, until the butter is absorbed.

Separately melt 1 tablespoon butter and add 2½ cups of the milk, already mixed with the cornstarch. Cook well, stirring constantly to avoid lumps. When thick and creamy, add 3 egg yolks which have been beaten with the remaining ½ cup milk. Add the cooked shrimp and onion, and put this mixture in a buttered casserole covered with beaten egg whites, which have been lightly salted, and sprinkle with the grated cheese and bread crumbs. Brown in a 400-degree oven for about 20 minutes.

78. Shrimp Omelet (Fritada)

   45 minutes
   1 pound fresh shrimp, cleaned
   3 tablespoons oil
   1 onion, chopped
   1 teaspoon salt
   1 dash cayenne pepper
   3 small tomatoes, peeled and chopped
   ¾ cup or 1 can coconut milk
   6 eggs, beaten
   1 teaspoon vinegar
   butter
   6 servings

Fry shrimp in oil with onion, salt, pepper, and tomatoes. Gradually add the coconut milk, stirring slowly. Cool, mix with the eggs, to which the vinegar has been added after beating, and put in buttered casserole. Bake in a 350-degree oven for 10 to 15 minutes, or until eggs are cooked.

79. SHRIMP FRIGIDEIRA *free-gee-day'-rah*
(Frigideira de Camarões)

A *frigideira* is a baked dish which always has eggs baked on the top. It is made of meat, fish, or vegetables.

1½ hours
½ pound salt codfish
½ pound dried shrimp
1½ onions
1 pinch garlic powder
1 dash pepper
1 teaspoon paprika
¾ cup coconut milk
2 tablespoons oil
½ teaspoon vinegar
4 eggs, beaten
1 teaspoon flour
8 olives, pitted and chopped
6 servings

Soak codfish overnight and the next day remove skin and bones, and grind shrimp and codfish together. Mix with this 1 onion, minced, garlic powder, pepper, and paprika. Add coconut milk, oil, and vinegar. Mix well and cook 20 minutes. Beat 2 eggs, stir in the flour, olives, and ½ onion, chopped. Combine this with the first mixture, spread in a rather wide baking pan, and cover with the remaining 2 well-beaten eggs, and brown in a 400-degree oven until eggs are well set, 10 to 15 minutes.

80. CRISPY DRIED SHRIMP PIES (Pasteis de Camarão)

    1 hour 15 minutes
1 tablespoon butter
1 cup flour
1 dash salt
1 cup milk
1 basic recipe Shrimp Sauce (Recipe 40)
3 eggs, beaten
2 cups dry bread crumbs
oil for frying
    8 servings

Make a dough as follows: work butter into the flour, add salt, and gradually add milk, mixing until smooth. Cook in a heavy saucepan until very thick. Cool. Roll on a floured board to ¼ inch thickness. Cut dough with a 3-inch round cooky cutter. Place a spoonful of the Shrimp Sauce on each, fold over, and press edges together with fork to close tightly. Dip each pie in beaten eggs and coat with bread crumbs. Fry in hot oil until brown. Serve hot.

81. BRAZILIAN EMPADINHA *em-pa-deen'-ya*
(Empadinhas Brasileiras)

These little pies are especially tasty. Make them in your large muffin tins, and serve hot for a luncheon dish. The crust is very tender and crumbly. If you wish to serve them as an appetizer, or along with salads and sandwiches for supper, as we do in Brazil, make them in the smallest muffin tins you can find.

> 1 hour 15 minutes
>
> ¾ cup butter
> 2 cups flour
> 1½ teaspoons salt
> 7 egg yolks
> ½ pound fresh shrimp, cleaned
> 1 teaspoon salt
> 1 cup milk
> 1 tablespoon flour
> 1 teaspoon onion juice
> 4 tablespoons grated cheese
> 8 olives, pitted
> 8 large servings

Work the butter into the flour, as for pie dough; add 3 lightly beaten egg yolks and ½ teaspoon salt. Roll out small balls of this pastry and press into 8 large-size muffin tins. The dough is crumbly —you may press it into the tins without rolling if you find that is easier. Cook shrimp in salted water, barely enough to cover, and chop fine. Add milk, mixed with the flour, onion juice, 3 beaten egg yolks, and cheese. Taste for salt. Fill shells with this mixture and add a pitted olive to each. Cover each with dough and press the edges together. Brush tops with the remaining egg yolk to give a shiny glaze. Bake in a 350-degree oven for 20 to 30 minutes, or until brown. Note: You may add drained canned peas to the filling, or even a very small quantity of finely chopped cooked carrot.

82. IMPERIAL CROWN (Corôa Imperial)

  1 hour

  2 cups rice
  4 cups water
  1 teaspoon salt
  bread crumbs
  12 large shrimps, cleaned
  1 basic recipe Shrimp Sauce (Recipe 40)
  2 tablespoons butter
  ¼ tablespoon salt
  2 green peppers, cut in rings
  2 sweet red peppers, cut in rings
  1 cucumber, sliced
    6 to 8 servings

Cook the rice in the water and salt and turn into a round greased baking dish lined with bread crumbs. Let dry in 300-degree oven, and turn onto a hot dish. Have ready the Shrimp Sauce. Fry the large shrimp in the butter and salt. Arrange the fried shrimp on the rice mold, surround with hot Shrimp Sauce, and garnish with rings of green and red pepper and sliced cucumber.

83. SHRIMP GELATIN WITH LOBSTER MAYONNAISE (Gelatina de Camarão e Lagosta

2 hours

2 pounds fresh shrimp
2 tablespoons lemon juice
2 cups water
2 cups white wine
2 carrots, sliced
1 bay leaf
1 clove garlic, minced
1 teaspoon salt
2 envelopes unflavored gelatin
2 egg whites, beaten
3 tablespoons butter
2 lobsters, or 2 large cans lobster meat
2 teaspoons salt
caraway seeds
lettuce
2 cups well-seasoned mayonnaise
8 to 10 servings

Shell the shrimp, remove heads, clean, and let soak in lemon juice. Cook heads and shells in 1 cup water and the wine, adding carrots, bay leaf, garlic, and 1 teaspoon salt. Simmer for 40 minutes. Strain through a damp cloth. Sprinkle gelatin on 1 cup cold water and leave until water is absorbed. Return shrimp and wine broth to flame, and add gelatin, stirring until dissolved. Remove from flame. Add the 2 beaten egg whites and let stand for ½ hour to clear; then strain through a damp cloth. In the meantime, fry the shrimp in 2 tablespoons butter and cool. Put 1 inch of the gelatin mixture in a mold, and put in refrigerator to set, then add some shrimps and cover with another inch of gelatin, cooling and repeating until you have used up all the gelatin and shrimp. Return to refrigerator to set and chill thoroughly. Cook the lobsters as follows: fill a large pan with water, and put in salt and the caraway seeds in a bag. When water starts to boil, put in lobsters and cook for 12 to 15 minutes. Drain, add 1 tablespoon butter to the lobsters, and shake over fire until butter is absorbed. Remove meat from shells. Mix this lobster meat, or the canned lobster meat, with the mayonnaise. Unmold shrimp gelatin onto large plate, surround with lobster mayonnaise, garnish with lettuce leaves, and decorate with lobster heads and tails.

84. SHRIMP PIE (Torta de Camarão Maranhense) from Maranhão

1 pound fresh shrimp, washed
salt
1 pound dried shrimp, cleaned
3 tablespoons olive oil
1 medium-sized onion, chopped
2 small tomatoes, peeled, seeded, and chopped
1 small green pepper, chopped
4 medium-sized potatoes
7 eggs
cayenne pepper (optional)
  6 servings

Remove heads and shells from the fresh shrimp and put on to boil in a small quantity of water with a little salt. Cook for 20 minutes, strain, and save the broth (there should be about 1 cup). Grind the dried shrimp. Put the oil in a heavy pan, add the cleaned shrimps, the onion, tomatoes, and green pepper. Cook slowly, but do not fry. Cook the potatoes. Add the ground dried shrimp and the shrimp broth to the cooked shrimp mixture, simmer for 10 minutes, slice in the potatoes, and cook all together until rather dry. Taste for salt. Remove from fire, and cool enough so that when 4 of the eggs have been beaten and stirred into this mixture, they will not cook. Put into a greased round baking dish (large pie pan or something similar). Beat the other 3 eggs, add a little salt and pepper, and pour on top. Bake in hot oven until eggs are set. Serve hot, cut in wedges.

85. SHRIMP WITH CHAYOTE (Camarão com Chuchu) from Recife

1 hour

1 pound fresh shrimp
2 tablespoons olive oil
1 small tomato, peeled and chopped
1 small onion, chopped
1 teaspoon salt
2 large chayotes
½ cup coconut milk
1 dash cayenne pepper
4 servings

Clean the shrimp and cook the heads and shells with a small amount of water for 20 minutes. Strain and reduce the broth to ½ cup. Make a *refogado* of the oil, tomato, onion, and salt, add cleaned shrimp, cook for 5 minutes, add shrimp broth, and cook for 5 minutes more. Peel and cut the chayotes in large chunks, cook in a small amount of water for 5 minutes. Add to shrimp mixture with the coconut milk and cayenne pepper. Cook until chayote is tender. Serve hot with Fluffy Rice (Recipe 137) or Rice with Coconut Milk (Recipe 136).

POULTRY

The next time you have a nice young duck to cook, try one of these recipes. The simple Roast Duck with Oranges (Recipe 87), or the marinated, pot-roasted Rio Grande Duck with Stuffed Peaches (Recipe 88), the Christmas Duck (Recipe 89), or Baked Duck with Apples and Giblet Croquettes (Recipe 90)—take your choice, any one will be a happy surprise for your family and friends. Baked Chicken, Country Style (Recipe 92) is the favorite dish of one of Brazil's famous surgeons, and Chicken with Cheese Sauce and Peas (Recipe 94) was served at the buffet dinner of a famous hostess. Turkey is a must for any important dinner in Brazil, and the recipe for Stuffed Turkey, Brazilian Style (Recipe 98) has appeared on the table at many fashionable international dinner parties. The last recipe, Giblets Baked with Rice and Cheese (Recipe 100), is almost always served as one of the dishes at buffet suppers, and usually appears at Sunday home luncheons.

86. Duck with Tucupi Sauce *too-coo-ped*
(Pato no Tucupi)

1½ hours
- 1 duck, 4 to 5 pounds
- 2 cloves garlic, minced
- 1 tablespoon salt
- 1 tablespoon chopped parsley
- 1 tablespoon chives
- 1 cup vinegar
- 3 tablespoons butter
- 3 cups water
  6 servings

Clean duck and soak overnight in garlic, salt, parsley, chives, and vinegar. The following day, drain, and brown the duck in the butter. Then add the water, little by little, cooking until the duck becomes tender. The Tucupi Sauce (below) is prepared the day before.

TUCUPI SAUCE

1½ cups water
2 pounds manioc flour
1 pinch cayenne pepper

Pour the water over the manioc flour, stirring to prevent lumps. Put in a cloth bag, drain. Store the liquid in the refrigerator until the following day. When the duck has cooked tender, pour this liquid over it, and add the pinch of cayenne pepper. Cook for 20 minutes. The sauce should be thin. Serve with plain manioc flour or bread crumbs.

87. ROAST DUCK WITH ORANGES (Pato Assado com Laranjas)

2 hours

1 young duck, 4 to 5 pounds
1 cup wine
1 clove garlic, minced
juice of 1 lemon
1 tablespoon chopped parsley
1 teaspoon salt
1 tablespoon chopped chives or green-onion tops
3 tablespoons butter
2 teaspoons salt
orange juice
6 oranges, peeled and sliced
    6 to 8 servings

Clean the duck and marinate overnight in wine, garlic, lemon juice, parsley, salt, and chives or green-onion tops. The following day, drain, rub with butter, and sprinkle salt over top and inside. Roast, uncovered, in 350-degree oven for 1½ hours, or until done, basting with orange juice. Serve whole on hot platter garnished with oranges.

88. Rio Grande Duck with Stuffed Peaches (Pato ao Rio Grande)

    3 hours
    1 young duck, 4 to 5 pounds
    1 cup wine
    1 clove garlic, minced
    juice of 1 lemon
    1 tablespoon chopped parsley
    1 tablespoon chopped chives or green-onion tops
    2 teaspoons salt
    3 tablespoons butter
    ½ cup water
    duck giblets
    ½ pound ham, cooked and minced
    1 cup thick standard-recipe white sauce
    16 peach halves
    ½ cup grated cheese
    1 cup cream
    lettuce
    6 to 8 servings

Clean duck and marinate overnight in wine, garlic, lemon juice, parsley, chives or green-onion tops, and 1 teaspoon salt. Next day, drain duck, put butter in heavy kettle, and brown duck on all sides. Add ½ cup water and 1 teaspoon salt and cook, tightly covered, adding a little water as necessary. Cook the giblets in a little salted water. Drain, and use broth as part of the liquid in which to cook the duck. Add minced giblets and ham to white sauce. Drain peach halves well, fill each one with the minced-giblet-ham-white-sauce mixture, sprinkle with grated cheese, and brown in a 400-degree oven for 15 minutes. When duck is thoroughly cooked (about 1½ hours), pour cream over it, heat, but do not boil. Carve the duck and arrange on hot platter, surrounded with peach halves, pour sauce in kettle over duck, decorate platter with lettuce leaves.

89. CHRISTMAS DUCK (Pato de Natal)

2½ hours

1 young duck, 4 to 5 pounds
1 cup wine
1 clove garlic, minced
juice of 1 lemon
2 teaspoons salt
1 tablespoon chopped parsley
1 tablespoon chopped chives or green-onion tops
duck giblets
1 tablespoon butter
1 dash nutmeg
1 dash pepper
½ pound chestnuts, boiled and chopped
¼ pound bacon
¼ pound salt pork
  8 servings

Soak duck overnight in wine, garlic, lemon juice, 1 teaspoon salt, parsley, and chives or green onions. Next day, drain and wipe thoroughly and fill with the following stuffing: chop the giblets, mix with melted butter, nutmeg, pepper, chestnuts, and 1 teaspoon salt. Wrap in aluminum foil, first placing slices of bacon and salt pork over breast. Roast in a 375-degree oven for 1½ hours, test to see if tender, remove foil, and serve whole on hot platter.

90. BAKED DUCK WITH APPLES AND GIBLET CROQUETTES (Pato Assado com Maçã e Croquetes de Miudos)

3 hours

1 young duck, 3 to 4 pounds
2 cups white wine
1 clove garlic, minced
1 tablespoon salt
1 dash pepper
3 tablespoons butter
  6 servings

Marinate the duck overnight in white wine, garlic, salt, and pepper. Drain, rub with butter, and roast in oven for 1½ hours at 400 degrees, or until done.

GIBLET CROQUETTES

Duck giblets
1 small onion, finely minced
1 small tomato, peeled, seeded, and chopped
1 cup thick, well-seasoned standard-recipe white sauce
3 eggs
bread crumbs
oil for frying

Cook giblets in small amount of salted water until tender, chop, add onion and tomato, fold this into white sauce, make into croquettes, dip in beaten eggs and bread crumbs. Fry in hot oil until golden brown.

PREPARATION OF APPLES

6 apples
6 teaspoons butter

Core apples, but without breaking through to bottom. Place a teaspoon of butter in each cavity and wrap apples tightly in squares of aluminum-foil. Place in a pan with a little water in the bottom and bake for ½ hour at 375 degrees. When done, open corners of paper to form a flower. Put the duck in center of platter and surround with croquettes and apples.

91. CHICKEN COOKED IN MILK (Galinha com Leite)

2½ hours

1 chicken, 5 pounds
½ cup vinegar
juice of 1 lemon
1 tablespoon salt
1 dash pepper
1 dash cayenne pepper
1 tablespoon chopped parsley
1 tablespoon chopped chives
1 clove garlic
3 small onions
1 bay leaf
3 tablespoons butter
4 cups milk
  6 to 8 servings

Disjoint chicken and marinate overnight in vinegar, lemon juice, salt, pepper, cayenne pepper, parsley, chives, garlic, onion, and bay leaf. Next day, drain and dry chicken. Brown in butter, add the marinade, add milk, cover, and cook over low heat until tender. Should milk evaporate before chicken is done, add a little more.

92. BAKED CHICKEN, COUNTRY STYLE
(Galinha com Arroz à Camponêza)

4 hours

1 fat chicken, 5 pounds
½ cup vinegar
1 clove garlic, minced
1 tablespoon salt
2 tablespoons butter
½ cup white wine
6 small tomatoes
6 hard-cooked eggs
1 cup chopped olives
6 slices ham, chopped
3 tablespoons chopped dill pickles
1 basic recipe Fluffy Rice (Recipe 137)
2 cups grated Parmesan cheese
    8 to 10 servings

Soak chicken overnight in vinegar, garlic, and salt. Next day brown the chicken in 1 tablespoon butter, add wine and some water almost to cover. Cover and cook, adding water if necessary. When tender, cool and remove bones. Boil the bones for ½ hour in the same liquid in which the chicken was cooked, remove bones, add the tomatoes to liquid. Cook for 25 minutes and strain. Add the other tablespoon of butter, 5 eggs, mashed, ¾ cup olives, ham, and pickles, pour over chicken and return to flame and cook a few minutes. Grease a casserole and put in layers of chicken and rice alternately, sprinkling each layer with grated cheese. Top layer should be of cheese. Garnish with 1 sliced egg and more chopped olives, and brown for 15 minutes in a 350-degree oven.

93. CHICKEN CROQUETTES (Croquetes de Galinha)

2 hours

1 chicken, 3 pounds
2 tablespoons butter
salt
4 slices white bread
½ cup milk
4 eggs
1 dash pepper
bread crumbs
oil for frying
    8 servings

Brown chicken in butter, add enough water with salt to cook tender. Remove bones and put the meat through grinder. Cut crusts from bread and soak pulp in milk, adding to the chicken meat. Mix in 2 eggs and pepper. Place over low heat and cook until dry. Make small croquettes and dip in 2 beaten eggs, then in bread crumbs. Fry in hot oil and serve at once.

94. CHICKEN WITH CHEESE SAUCE AND PEAS (Galinha com Creme de Ervilhas)

1½ hours

1 chicken, 3 pounds
salt
3 tablespoons butter
1 small onion, chopped
1 clove garlic, minced
2 small tomatoes, peeled and chopped
2 tablespoons flour
½ cup cream
1 tablespoon butter
2 egg yolks, beaten
1 tablespoon grated Parmesan cheese
3 cups canned peas
    6 servings

Disjoint chicken and season with salt. Cook in a *refogado* of butter, onion, garlic, and tomatoes. Add water and cook until tender. Remove from stove, strain, and save the stock. Make a sauce of the flour, cream, butter, and the stock (about 1 cup). Add the beaten eggs, Parmesan cheese, and peas, heat well, stirring, until thick, and pour over chicken and serve.

95. PARMESAN CHICKEN (Frango ao Parmesão)

1½ hours

2 frying chickens, 2 pounds each
⅓ cup butter
2 teaspoons salt
¼ teaspoon pepper
1 teaspoon paprika
2½ cups grated Parmesan cheese
2 cups white wine
1 level tablespoon mustard
2 cups cream
1 cup soft bread crumbs
8 servings

Disjoint the chicken, melt the butter in a heavy pan, and add chicken. Sprinkle with salt, pepper, and paprika and let brown slowly, tightly covered. When chicken is browned and cooked through, arrange the pieces in a greased ovenproof dish. In the juice that is left in the pan, mix 2 cups grated cheese, let it melt, add wine, mustard, and the cream. Let it come to a boil, stirring all the time. Taste for salt. Pour this over the chicken, sprinkle with the bread crumbs and grated cheese. Put in a hot oven for 10 minutes to brown.

96. MINAS STEWED CHICKEN (Ensopado de Galinha à Mineira)

1½ hours

1 young chicken, 4 pounds
3 tablespoons lard
1 pound tomatoes, peeled and chopped
2 tablespoons chopped parsley
1 clove garlic, minced
1 tablespoon salt
3 tablespoons onion, chopped
1 pound potatoes, peeled and cut in large pieces
3 large carrots, sliced
3 cups water
6 servings

Disjoint the chicken. Put the lard in a heavy pan, and, when hot, add the chicken and let it brown. Then add the tomatoes, parsley, garlic, salt, onion, potatoes, and carrots. Add the water, cover well, and let cook until chicken and vegetables are tender and juice is almost absorbed. Serve in wide, deep dish.

97. CHICKEN VATAPÁ *vah-tah-pah'* (Vatapá de Galinha)

4 hours

1 pound dried shrimp
2 pounds fresh shrimp
juice of 2 lemons
1 chicken, 3 or 4 pounds
2 tablespoons lard
1 large onion, chopped
3 tomatoes, peeled and chopped
1 clove garlic, minced
1 tablespoon salt
2 tablespoons peanut butter
1½ cups coconut milk
½ cup *dendê*, corn, or peanut oil
6 to 8 servings

Soak dried shrimp overnight; next day, clean and grind. Clean fresh shrimp and marinate in lemon juice. Disjoint chicken and fry in a *refogado* of lard, onion, tomatoes, garlic, and salt. Add a little water and simmer, adding more water as needed, until chicken is tender. Remove from sauce, and take meat from bones and cut into small pieces. Strain the sauce and add the ground dried shrimp, the drained fresh shrimp, the peanut butter, coconut milk, and *dendê* oil. Cook until thick and serve with following sauce:

SAUCE

> 3 tablespoons rice flour
> 1 cup milk
> ¾ cup coconut milk
> 2 tablespoons oil

Mix rice flour with milk and coconut milk, cook until thick, and add oil, little by little. Cool and serve over *vatapá*.

98. STUFFED TURKEY, BRAZILIAN STYLE (Perú à Brasileira)

> 5 hours

1 turkey, 10 to 12 pounds
salt
½ pound pork
3 slices ham
turkey giblets
1 tablespoon chopped parsley
1 tablespoon chives
2 tablespoons oil
1 small onion, chopped
1 clove garlic, minced
1 teaspoon salt
1 teaspoon dried hot pepper
3 hard-cooked eggs, diced
4 slices white bread
½ cup white wine
3 tablespoons butter
2 tablespoons dry bread crumbs
3 slices bacon
> 8 to 10 servings

Prepare the turkey, rub with salt. Chop the pork, ham, and giblets and cook in a *refogado* of parsley, chives, oil, onion, garlic, salt, and pepper, until tender. Add the hard-cooked eggs. Soak bread in wine and add to the *refogado* along with 1 tablespoon butter and the dry bread crumbs. Mix thoroughly. Stuff the turkey with this mixture and sew up. Cover breast with bacon slices, spread with butter, and wrap in aluminum foil. Roast for 3½ to 4 hours at 375 degrees, or until perfectly tender. You may add chestnuts to the stuffing if you like. Serve with Sarrabulho (Recipe 99).

99. SARRABULHO (*sar-rah-bool'-yo*)

To be served with roast turkey or other fowl.

   1½ hours

   2 pounds prunes
   1 pound white raisins
   2 cups white wine
   1 pound turkey giblets
   salt
   1 tablespoon margarine
   1 onion, grated
   pepper
   2 cups fresh bread cut in cubes
   ½ cup milk
      8 servings

Cook prunes and raisins until tender in wine and enough water to cover. Cook giblets until tender in a little salted water, cut in small pieces, and fry in a *refogado* of margarine, onion, salt, and pepper. Soak bread cubes in milk, then press through a sieve and add to the *refogado*. Finally mix in the fruit and juice. If necessary thicken with a little flour to make a fairly thick sauce.

100. Giblets Baked with Rice and Cheese (Arroz de Fôrno)

1½ hours

½ pound chicken giblets
3 cups chicken broth
1 onion, chopped
2 small tomatoes, peeled
1 clove garlic, minced
1 tablespoon chopped parsley
1½ cups rice, uncooked
1 tablespoon butter
3 hard-cooked eggs, chopped
3 cups peas, cooked
½ cup whole small olives
grated Parmesan cheese
   6 servings

Cook giblets in a little of the chicken broth with onion, tomatoes, garlic, and half the parsley for 20 minutes. Brown rice in butter, add chicken broth and the giblet mixture. When the broth is absorbed and rice is tender, remove from flame, add eggs, peas, olives, and remaining parsley. Spread on a wide ovenproof dish and sprinkle generously with grated Parmesan cheese. Bake for 20 minutes at 350 degrees.

MEATS

Brazil's fertile lands produce many thousands of head of cattle every year for home consumption and for export. Meat is an important article of diet, and substitute dishes are seldom used, since it is plentiful and relatively cheap. Except for religious fast days, meat appears on the table twice a day, and sometimes two separate meat dishes are served at the same meal. From the Stuffed Suckling Pig (Recipe 106), Pot Roast with Oranges (Recipe 111), and meat-filled Stuffed Pancakes, rich with melted cheese (Recipe 103), you will find a recipe for any occasion. Try plain thick Beef Tenderloin with Farofa (Recipe 101) or the delicious Milanesas (Recipe 104), or give your family or guests a treat with the Pork Chop Croquettes (Recipe 105).

101. BEEF TENDERLOIN WITH FAROFA
far-off'-ah (Filé Mignon com Farofa)

2 hours 20 minutes

1 beef tenderloin
¼ cup olive oil
juice of 1 lemon
1½ teaspoons salt
1 basic recipe Farofa (Recipe 56)
parsley
lemon slices
6 servings

Cut beef tenderloin in slices 1¼ inch in thickness, across the grain. Marinate for several hours in the olive oil, lemon juice, and salt. Remove from marinade and put on grill, and grill until brown on one side, turn over, baste with marinade, and finish cooking. The length of time depends on the rareness desired. Put on one end of a very hot platter, pile the *farofa* on the other end of platter, garnish with sprig of parsley and lemon slices. Serve quickly so that it is very hot.

102. SMOTHERED BEEF TENDERLOIN (Filé Mignon Refogado)

2½ hours

¼ cup olive oil
4 tablespoons of good vinegar
2 teaspoons salt
1 beef tenderloin
1 cup chopped onion
1 cup finely cubed raw carrots
6 servings

Make a marinade of the olive oil, vinegar, and salt, and soak meat for 2 hours. Heat a large heavy frying pan, put the whole tenderloin in the pan with the marinade, the onion, and the carrots. Cover and cook, turning the meat now and then, being careful that the flame is not too high. When the carrots are tender and the meat brown, remove meat to hot platter and pour the carrot-and-onion mixture that is left in the pan over the meat. The meat should still be rather rare inside. The olive oil and vinegar with vegetables is a delicious combination with the tender beef.

103. Stuffed Pancakes (Panquecas Recheadas)

1 hour 15 minutes

3 tablespoons butter
1 tablespoon chopped onion
¼ clove garlic, finely minced
1 small tomato, peeled and seeded
½ cup chopped mushrooms
salt
pepper
1 tablespoon chopped parsley
gravy or bouillon
3 cups ground cooked veal or pork
  6 servings

Put the butter in a frying pan, melt, add onion, garlic, tomato, mushrooms, salt, pepper, and parsley. Cook all together for a few minutes, add a little gravy or bouillon, and cook until onions are soft. Mix in meat. Make the following pancakes:

3 egg yolks
1½ teaspoons melted butter, cooled
¼ teaspoon salt
1 teaspoon sugar
6 tablespoons flour
¾ cup milk
3 egg whites, well beaten
grated Parmesan cheese

Beat the egg yolks, add the cooled melted butter, salt, sugar, and flour, beating constantly. Add the milk, mix well, and fold in the well-beaten egg whites. Make 12 thin pancakes of this mixture. Put a spoonful of meat mixture on each pancake, roll up and tuck in ends, and put in ovenproof dish. Sprinkle thickly with grated cheese, and put in hot oven to melt and brown the cheese. Serve in baking dish, very hot.

104. MILANESAS (*mee-lan-ay'-zas*)

45 minutes
1 pound veal steak cut in individual servings ½ inch thick
garlic
salt
pepper
2 eggs
4 tablespoons water
fine, dry bread crumbs
oil for sautéing
Lemon Sauce (Recipe 124)
4 servings

Pound the steaks, rub each with a piece of cut garlic, salt, and pepper. Beat the eggs, add water. Roll steaks in bread crumbs, then dip in egg, and again in crumbs. Let dry for ½ hour. Sauté in hot oil until brown on both sides. Serve on hot platter, accompanied by Lemon Sauce.

105. PORK CHOP CROQUETTES (Costeletas de Porco)

1 hour
about ⅓ cup seasoned mashed potato for each pork chop
salt
pepper
pork chops, cut 1 inch thick
oil for frying
fine, dry bread crumbs
eggs
lemon slices
parsley

Prepare the mashed potatoes (not too soft) and cool. Salt and pepper each pork chop and fry in oil, covering the pan and adding a few tablespoons of water to steam well, so as to be sure the pork is well cooked. Remove from pan, cool a little. Coat the meaty part of the pork chop with a thick layer of the mashed potato, roll each in bread crumbs, beaten egg, and again in bread crumbs. Have oil in pan about 1 inch deep. Brown the chops on both sides in the hot oil. Serve on hot platter, garnished with lemon slices and parsley.

106. STUFFED SUCKLING PIG (Leitão Recheado)

5 hours

1 suckling pig
1 cup vinegar
1 cup red wine
2 cloves garlic
3 bay leaves
1 tablespoon salt
1 tablespoon cloves
1½ teaspoons pepper
½ teaspoon dried hot pepper
2 tablespoons lard or drippings
1 slice uncooked ham
4 pork sausages, finely chopped
1 onion, chopped
1 tablespoon chopped parsley
1 cup dry bread crumbs or manioc flour
1 cup pitted olives
2 hard-cooked eggs, chopped
6 slices smoked bacon
lemon slices
water cress
8 to 10 servings

Clean pig and soak 12 hours in vinegar, wine, 1 garlic clove, minced, bay leaves, salt, cloves, and pepper. Turn occasionally to allow seasonings to penetrate thoroughly. Heat fat in frying pan and add ham and sausages, and cook, adding water as needed until tender. Add onion, the other garlic clove, minced, and parsley. Fry, and mix in bread crumbs or manioc flour, stirring constantly. Do not let mixture get too dry. Remove from stove and add olives and eggs. Stuff the pig with this mixture, sew up, place in a roaster, and cover with bacon slices. Roast for 2½ hours at 350 degrees, or until done. Garnish with slice of lemon and sprigs of water cress.

107. ROAST LEG OF PORK (Pernil de Porco)

    4 hours

1 leg of fresh pork, 8 to 10 pounds
½ cup white wine
½ cup vinegar
juice of 1 lemon
2 cloves garlic, minced
2 bay leaves
½ tablespoon chopped parsley
½ tablespoon chopped chives
2 onions, chopped
½ teaspoon pepper
½ teaspoon hot pepper
2 tablespoons salt
2 green peppers, sliced
2 tablespoons bock beer
    8 to 10 servings

Soak pork overnight in wine, vinegar, lemon juice, garlic, bay leaves, parsley, chives, onions, pepper, salt, green peppers, and beer. Next day, roast in oven for about 3½ hours, or until tender, pouring liquid with seasoning over pork, and basting it occasionally.

108. BRAZILIAN CHOPPED MEAT (Picadinho à Brasileira)

    1 hour

2 pounds beef or pork
2 tablespoons lard
1 onion, chopped
2 small tomatoes, peeled and chopped
½ teaspoon chopped parsley
1 tablespoon chopped chives
1 clove garlic, minced
2 teaspoons salt
1½ cups water
3 hard-cooked eggs, sliced
½ cup pitted green olives
    4 to 6 servings

Chop beef or pork very fine, brown in a *refogado* of lard, onion, tomatoes, parsley, chives, garlic, and salt. Add 1 cup water and cook until meat and vegetables are tender and dry; add ½ cup water, if necesary, during cooking. Serve garnished with slices of hard-cooked eggs and olives.

109. CHOPPED MEAT, BAHIA STYLE
(Picadinho à Baiana)

1 hour

1 pound round steak
1 tablespoon lard
1 small onion, chopped
½ teaspoon chives, chopped
1 clove garlic, minced
1 dash pepper
1 teaspoon salt
1 tablespoon lemon juice
3 tablespoons *dendê* or olive oil
4 servings

Cut meat in small pieces and add to a *refogado* of lard, onion, chives, garlic, and pepper. Cover and cook for ½ hour. While cooking, add the salt and lemon juice and *dendê* or olive oil gradually. This dish is usually served with the following *"farofa"*:

½ cup *dendê*, peanut, or corn oil
2 cups dry bread crumbs
1 teaspoon salt
1 small onion, finely chopped

Mix oil and bread crumbs. Add salt and cook, stirring constantly, until dry. Stir in onion and serve with chopped meat.

110. STUFFED BEEF, BRAZILIAN STYLE
(Bife Recheado com Farofa)

1½ hours

2 pounds round beef, cut into 6 steaks
2 teaspoons salt
2 tablespoons vinegar
1 clove garlic, minced
2 small onions
½ teaspoon pepper
1 cup dry bread crumbs
2 tablespoons butter
2 hard-cooked eggs, chopped
½ cup pitted olives
3 tablespoons bacon fat
2 cups water
3 tomatoes
2 tablespoons port wine
6 servings

Slit each steak part way with a knife, so that it can be stuffed. Season with salt, 1 tablespoon vinegar, garlic, 1 chopped onion, and pepper. Separately, mix the bread crumbs with the butter, eggs, and olives. Stuff steaks with this mixture and secure edges with toothpicks. Heat the bacon fat in a pan; when hot, add the steaks, and brown well on both sides. Add water, cook until meat is tender, adding tomatoes and 1 sliced onion ½ hour before done. Pour 1 tablespoon vinegar and the port wine over the steaks, heat, and serve.

111. Pot Roast with Oranges (Carne Assada com Laranja)

4 hours

3 pounds chuck roast
juice of 1 lemon
2 teaspoons salt
6 slices bacon
1 clove garlic, minced
1 small onion, chopped
3 small tomatoes, peeled and chopped
1 bay leaf
1 dash pepper
2 cups orange juice
6 servings

Season meat with lemon juice and salt. Fry the bacon, remove from pan, and fry meat in bacon fat until golden brown. Add garlic, onion, tomatoes, bay leaf, and pepper. Cook for a few minutes and pour orange juice over meat. Cover and cook over low heat, until meat is tender. Should the liquid get too thick, add some more orange juice. When tender, remove meat and strain gravy. Garnish meat with bacon slices. Serve with boiled potatoes.

112. Brazilian Stew (Cozido à Brasileira)

3 hours

2 pounds beef for boiling
1 tablespoon vinegar
1 teaspoon salt
1 dash pepper
1 clove garlic, minced
1 onion, chopped
3 tablespoons lard or drippings
3 turnips, cut in pieces
3 carrots
2 large sweet potatoes, cut in pieces
4 large potatoes
1 cabbage, cut in sections
8 ears sweet corn
8 servings

Cut meat into pieces and soak in vinegar, salt, pepper, and garlic and onion for about 20 minutes. Put lard or drippings in a big heavy kettle, add the meat with all the seasonings. Cover with water, cook until almost tender, add turnips, carrots, sweet potatoes and other potatoes and cabbage and cook for ½ hour. Add sweet corn and cook for 10 minutes more. Serve with the following sauce:

SAUCE

1 small onion, chopped
2 tablespoons butter
½ cup bouillon
2 tablespoons grated cheese
1 dash cayenne pepper
flour
2 egg yolks, beaten

Fry onion in butter, add bouillon, cook slowly for a few minutes. Add cheese, pepper and enough flour to thicken well, and, last, the beaten egg yolks. The mixture should have the consistency of a purée. Arrange the meat and vegetables on a large platter, and serve accompanied by sauce.

113. TONGUE WITH RAISINS (Lingua com Passas)

5 hours

1 tongue
2 teaspoons salt
½ teaspoon pepper
1 clove garlic, minced
6 whole cloves
4 to 6 servings

Wash and scrape the tongue and boil in water with salt, pepper, garlic, and cloves, until tender. Peel. Cut in slices and serve with the following sauce:

SAUCE

- 2 tablespoons sugar
- 1 tablespoon vinegar
- 1 cup bouillon
- ½ cup raisins

Brown the sugar in heavy pan, add vinegar, bouillon, and raisins, and boil for a few minutes. Serve over slices of tongue.

114. TRIPE (Tripa)

3 hours

- 1 pound tripe
- 1 lemon
- 2 teaspoons salt
- 3 tablespoons shortening
- 1 small onion, chopped
- 1 clove garlic, minced
- ½ teaspoon chopped parsley
- ½ teaspoon chopped chives
- 2 small tomatoes, peeled and chopped
  4 servings

Wash tripe, rub with lemon, and soak in hot water for ½ hour. Drain thoroughly and boil in fresh water. When almost cooked, add salt. Make a *refogado* of fat, onion, garlic, parsley, chives, and tomatoes. Add the cooked tripe to the *refogado* and cook over low heat until tender. Serve garnished with chopped parsley.

115. ANGÚ MINEIRO *ang-goó meen-air'-o* (Angúr à Moda de Minas)

6 hours
½ pound liver
½ pound kidney
½ pound heart
½ pound fresh tongue
½ pound oxtail
vinegar
red wine
2 cloves garlic
1 bay leaf
6 whole cloves
1 teaspoon pepper
2 tablespoons bacon fat
1 teaspoon dried hot pepper
2 tablespoons chives
1 tablespoon salt
1 large onion, sliced
2 green peppers, sliced
2 tablespoons chopped parsley
3 pork sausages
1 tablespoon tomato paste
½ cup pitted olives
6 to 8 servings

Scald and chop meats in small pieces. Cover with equal parts vinegar and wine, 1 clove minced garlic, bay leaf, cloves, and pepper. Marinate for a few hours. Melt bacon fat and add 1 clove garlic, hot pepper, and chives. Add meats, brown and cover with plenty of water, and add the salt. When it begins to boil add onion slices, green-pepper slices, parsley, pieces of sausage, and tomato paste. Cook until all is tender; add olives. Serve with the following *angú:*

1 tablespoon bacon fat
1 small onion, chopped
3 cups water
1 teaspoon salt
corn meal

Make *refogado* with bacon fat and onion, add water and salt, bring to boil, sift in enough corn meal until mixture has the consistency of a very thick cream sauce.

SAUCES and GRAVIES

116. ANCHOVY SAUCE No. 1   (Môlho de Anchôvas) for fish

20 minutes

3 tablespoons butter
2 tablespoons flour
1 cup bouillon
2 egg yolks
2 teaspoons Anchovy Cream (Recipe 118)
few drops lemon juice
1 onion, chopped
1½ cups sauce

Brown 2 tablespoons butter with flour, add bouillon, saving 2 tablepoons, and cook until thick. Beat egg yolks with 2 tablespoons bouillon, strain, and add to first mixture. Add Anchovy Cream and lemon juice. Mix in the onion, browned in 1 tablespoon butter.

117. ANCHOVY SAUCE NO. 2 (Môlho de Anchôvas)

    20 minutes
  2 tablespoons butter
  2 tablespoons flour
  2 cups fish broth
  2 egg yolks, beaten
  1 tablespoon lemon juice
  1 medium-sized anchovy
  1 tablespoon oil
  1 small onion, grated
    2 cups sauce

Cook butter and flour until golden brown. Add fish broth, egg yolks, lemon juice, and the anchovy which has previously been pressed through a sieve. Cook, stirring well. Heat oil and sauté the onion. Add to the sauce. Serve hot with any kind of fish.

118. ANCHOVY CREAM (Creme de Anchôvas)

    15 minutes
  1 part anchovies
  2 parts butter

Clean anchovies, wash, and remove bones. Dry and mash with butter. Press through a sieve. You may use this for sandwich or canapé spread.

119. FISH SAUCE (Môlho para Peixe)

    ½ hour
  ½ cup water
  2 tablespoons vinegar
  1 dash salt
  1 dash pepper
  4 egg yolks
  2 tablespoons water
  3 tablespoons butter
  2 tablespoons cream
  few drops lemon juice
  salt
    1 cup sauce

Combine the ½ cup water with vinegar, salt, and pepper, and boil until reduced to half. Let cool. Mix egg yolks with 2 tablespoons water and add to liquid. Put into a double boiler and cook until thick, stirring constantly. Remove from flame. Add the butter and a few drops water, if necessary. Return to boiler and heat. Add the cream and lemon juice. Season with salt and beat well. Keep in double boiler until time to serve.

120. HERRING SAUCE (Môlho de Arenque) for fish

2 hours

1 herring
1 cup milk
2 tablespoons flour
2 tablespoons butter
½ onion, grated
1 bay leaf
3 slices lemon
3 cloves
6 whole black peppers
1 tablespoon lemon juice
1½ cups bouillon
1 tablespoon beef extract
few drops lemon juice
1 egg yolk, beaten
2 cups sauce

Soak herring in milk for 1 hour. Remove bones and cut in small pieces. Brown flour in butter, add onion, bay leaf, lemon slices, cloves, pepper, herring pieces, bouillon, and beef extract. Cook well, add lemon juice, and press through a sieve. Add beaten egg yolk mixed with a little of the sauce. Cook until thick. This sauce is also delicious with hot boiled potatoes.

121. CAPER SAUCE (Môlho de Alcaparras) for fish

    15 minutes
    2 tablespoons flour
    3 tablespoons butter
    1 cup fish broth
    1 tablespoon capers
    1 dash grated nutmeg
    1 dash black pepper
    few drops lemon juice
    1 egg yolk
    1¼ cups sauce

Brown flour in 2 tablespoons butter. Add fish broth and cook until thick. Remove from heat and add capers, nutmeg, pepper, lemon juice, egg yolk, and the remaining tablespoon butter. Heat again, but do not boil.

122. YELLOW SAUCE (Môlho Amarelo) for fish

    15 minutes
    3 hard-cooked eggs
    2 tablespoons butter
    2 cups fish broth
    2 teaspoons rice flour
    1 dash salt
    1 dash curry powder
    2½ cups sauce

Mash eggs and butter together until creamy and add the fish broth, little by little. Put on flame, stir constantly until mixture reaches the boiling point. Thicken with rice flour mixed with a little water. Season with salt and curry powder, boil a few minutes, and serve.

123. PICKLE SAUCE (Môlho de Pepino) for cooked meats

15 minutes

1 sour cucumber pickle
2 tablespoons butter
2 tablespoons flour
1 cup bouillon
3 tablespoons cream
  5 servings

Cut pickle very fine, in slices. Brown butter and flour, until golden brown. Add bouillon, cream, and cucumber slices and boil well.

124. LEMON SAUCE (Môlho de Limão) for breaded meats

15 minutes

1 tablespoon flour
3 tablespoons butter
½ cup white wine
½ cup water
1 lemon
1 dash salt
1 egg yolk, beaten
  1¼ cups sauce

Cook the flour in butter until golden brown. Add wine, water, grated rind and juice of lemon, and salt. Cook well, add beaten egg yolk, and serve.

125. CASANOVA SAUCE (Môlho Casanova) for cold meats

30 minutes

1 clove garlic, mashed
3 hard-cooked eggs
1 dash white pepper
1 teaspoon lemon juice
1 teaspoon salt
2 cups olive oil
some truffles
2½ cups sauce

Rub mashed garlic clove in a dish. Add egg yolks, pepper, lemon juice, and salt. Drop in olive oil, beating constantly, until thick. Chop the egg whites with the truffles and add to sauce.

126. MEAT GRAVY (Môlho de Carne)

20 minutes

1 small tomato, peeled and chopped
1 small onion, chopped
1 tablespoon meat drippings
1 cup juice from roasted meat or pot roast
¼ cup raisins
¼ cup pitted olives
½ cup water
1 tablespoon white wine
1½ cups gravy

Cook tomato and onion lightly in meat drippings, add the meat juice, raisins, olives, and water. Cook slowly for 10 minutes. Taste for salt. Add wine and serve in gravy boat with roasted or pot-roasted meat, or use it to heat slices of leftover meat.

127. TARTAR SAUCE (Môlho Tártaro)

10 minutes

2 tablespoons lemon juice
½ tablespoon sugar
½ onion, grated
chopped parsley
2 tablespoons chopped pickles
1 cup mayonnaise
1¼ cups sauce

Mix all ingredients together and beat thoroughly.

128. CARAMEL SAUCE (Môlho de Caramelo)

15 minutes

2 cups sugar
¼ cup butter
1 cup boiling water
1 tablespoon corn syrup
½ cup whipped cream
2 cups sauce

Put the sugar and butter in a heavy pan and brown lightly. It is not necessary for all the sugar to melt. Add the water slowly, add the corn syrup, and boil for 5 minutes. Cool and add whipped cream. Serve over puddings or frozen desserts.

129. PRUNE SAUCE (Môlho de Ameixa)

10 minutes

1 cup cooked sieved prunes
1 cup prune juice
1 cup sugar
juice of 1 lemon
½ cup chopped walnuts
2½ cups sauce

Mix all ingredients together and cook for 5 minutes. Serve over puddings or ice cream.

130. APPLE SAUCE   (Môlho de Maçã)

    20 minutes
    4 apples, peeled and cut in wedges
    2 cups water
    1 cup sugar
    1 tablespoon rum or port wine
    ¼ cup butter
      4 cups sauce

Cook the apples in the water until soft and slightly mushy, add sugar and rum or port wine, and cook for a few minutes more. Then add the butter and stir in well. Serve hot or cold with poultry or pork.

NOTE: See also Recipe 66 for ACARAJÉ SAUCE.

CHURRASCO

The *gaúcho* on the prairie kills the steer or animal to be barbecued, skins it, and cuts up the carcass. He cuts off a piece of the meat, preferably some ribs, puts it on the end of the spit, which is made of iron, and sticks the other end of the spit into the ground at such an angle that the meat hangs over the coals. It must not be too close; it must cook slowly without burning; and while it roasts, it is basted with a mixture of salt and water. The basting is done with a small leafy branch of a tree, or with a corn husk, or with a *chicolateira*—the iron tea kettle that the *gaúcho* uses over the fire. When the meat is brown and cooked, it is dipped into manioc flour. The *gaúcho* eats this with his fingers, skillfully cutting off a bite with a sharp knife as he secures the meat with his teeth.

In modern times, *churrasco* has become stylized. It is eaten with knife and fork and served at the table with a sauce made of onion, vinegar, and pepper. Such a sauce is never used on the range when the *churrasco* is cooked over the open fire. *Churrasco* is made of beef, pork, mutton, chicken, sausage, or *xarque* (*xarque* is meat that is salted and dried in the sun). We also eat *churrasco* at the *churrascarias* (special restaurants where the meat is roasted over charcoal). It is served with a sauce (Recipe 132), Farofa, which is a preparation of manioc flour (Recipe 56), hard French bread, and even fried potatoes and green salads.

We like to invite groups of friends to eat *churrasco* in our own back yards, or at our country homes or farms. Many times long tables are set up, with various condiments and plenty of beer and wine to accompany the meat. Cooks who are skilled in *churrasco* preparation are called in. Wood is used instead of charcoal, which gives the genuine *churrasco* flavor, delicately smoked, brown, and delicious.

131. RIO GRANDE CHURRASCO *shur-ras'-coe* (Churrasco à Rio Grande)

This recipe is for a large quantity of barbecue. You may use a variety of meats, such as beef tenderloin, some ribs of lamb, or even a whole lamb, cleaned and divided into large pieces, leg of lamb, ribs of beef or veal. The meat should be of the best quality, and tender.

> 2 to 4 hours (depending on cut of meat used) after fire is prepared
> 10 to 15 pounds of meat
> ½ cup salt
> 6 cloves of garlic, finely mashed
> 3 cups hot water
> 15 to 20 servings

Prepare your fire of charcoal or wood. For the genuine Rio Grande *churrasco*, it should be a wood fire. The coals should be bright before the meat is put on to roast. Spread the meat on the grill, but do not let the pieces touch. When the meat begins to brown, baste with the following: dissolve the salt in the hot water and add the garlic. Keep on basting until the meat is cooked. If you should run out of the basting liquid before the meat is cooked, prepare a little more. The meat should not be too close to the fire, or it may burn before it is cooked through. The garlic is optional, but even those who do not care for garlic will find that it gives a delicate extra flavor. When the meat is done to your taste, leave it over the fire, which will have died down somewhat, and cut off pieces to serve. A tender rib cut at just the right stage of brownness and juiciness, eaten with the fingers, will never be forgotten. Try dipping it into some Farofa (Recipe 56).

126

132. Sᾶo Paulo Churrasco *shur-ras'-coe* (Churrasco Paulista)

  1 hour

  2 pounds beef tenderloin
  3 teaspoons salt
  juice of 2 lemons
  ¼ teaspoon pepper
  1 dash dried hot pepper
  1 large onion, chopped
  ½ cup chopped parsley
    4 to 6 servings

Marinate the meat overnight in the juice of 1 lemon, salt, and pepper. Barbecue the meat, turning frequently. Serve with a sauce made from the juice of the remaining lemon, the hot pepper, the onion and parsley. You may also serve it with the following:

133. Banana Farofa *far-off'-ah* (Farofa de Banana)

  15 minutes

  6 bananas, cut in thick slices
  5 tablespoons butter
  1 large onion, cut in rings
  3 tablespoons dry bread crumbs

Fry bananas in butter until golden brown; remove from fat. Fry onion rings in the same butter. Add bananas, stir in bread crumbs, and brown. Do not let it get too dry—add a little more butter if necessary. The crumbs should be coated with butter, but light and loose. Serve hot.

134. MINAS CHURRASCO *shur-ras'-coe*   (Churrasco Mineiro)

1 hour

2 pounds beef tenderloin
juice of 1 lemon
3 teaspoons salt
1 clove garlic, mashed
4 to 6 servings

Marinate the meat overnight in the lemon juice, salt, and garlic. The next day, proceed as for São Paulo Churrasco (Recipe 132). Serve with or without sauce.

135. CHICKEN CHURRASCO *shur-ras'-coe* (Churrasco de Frango)

1 hour

young frying-size chickens (½ chicken per person)
1 teaspoon salt for each chicken
¼ cup olive oil for each chicken
1 clove garlic, minced (optional)

Clean the chickens, rub inside and out with the salt, and soak in the oil and garlic for 2 hours. Put on grill and roast slowly, turning and basting with the oil during roasting.

Everyone eats rice in Brazil, from the richest to the poorest, and when you have tried some of our typical rice dishes, you will see why. Cooking rice properly, so that every grain is separate, well cooked, but not sticky, is an art, and when onions and other seasonings are added, it is good enough to serve at a banquet (as is done in Brazil). You may enjoy using these rice recipes to serve with your own meat dishes.

136. Rice with Coconut Milk (Arroz com Leite de Côco) to serve with meat dishes

    35 minutes
- 2 cups rice
- ¾ teaspoon salt
- 2 cups boiling water
- ¾ cups coconut milk
- 4 servings

Wash rice and boil in salted water for 15 minutes. Add the coconut milk, continue cooking (covered) over low heat until thick, stirring very gently with a fork now and then. Press into a greased mold, then turn onto hot serving plate.

137. FLUFFY RICE (Arroz Simples)

½ hour

½ small onion, chopped
1 clove garlic, minced (optional)
2 tablespoons lard or vegetable fat
2 cups rice
3 to 4 cups boiling water
1 teaspoon salt
4 servings

Fry chopped onion and garlic in fat until light brown, add rice, cook for 2 or 3 minutes, stirring constantly. Add about 3 cups of boiling water and the salt, cook over low heat, until water is absorbed and rice is cooked. It may be necessary to add a little more boiling water as it cooks, but never stir the rice. When water is absorbed, lower flame, cover, and cook until rice is fluffy. With a little practice, you can make a delicious fluffy rice, with every grain separate.

138. BRAZILIAN RICE (Arroz Brasileiro)

½ hour

2 tablespoons lard or vegetable fat
1 small onion, chopped
½ clove garlic, minced (optional)
3 tomatoes, peeled and chopped
1 bay leaf
2 cups rice
1 teaspoon salt
3 or 4 cups boiling water
4 to 6 servings

Make a *refogado* with lard, onion, garlic, tomatoes, and bay leaf. Add rice and salt and stir until the rice absorbs the *refogado*. Cover with boiling water. Cook over high heat for 5 minutes, reduce heat, cover, and simmer. Cook until fluffy and tender. Should the rice become too dry before it is tender, add a small amount of boiling water.

139. RICE AND BANANAS WITH LEFTOVER MEAT (Arroz com Bananas)

1 hour

1 pound leftover pork or beef, ground and seasoned
Fluffy Rice (Recipe 137)
3 tablespoons butter
6 bananas, cut lengthwise
grated cheese
3 hard-cooked eggs, sliced
12 green olives, pitted
   6 servings

Place alternate layers of meat and rice in a greased casserole, finishing with layer of rice. Dot with butter, cover with a layer of bananas, sprinkle with grated cheese, and dot again with butter. Bake for about 20 minutes in a 375-degree oven. Garnish with hard-cooked eggs and green olives.

140. CARIOCA RICE WITH CHICKEN (Arroz Carioca)

1½ hours

6 slices bacon
1 small frying chicken, cut in pieces
1 onion, chopped
1 tablespoon salt
2 tomatoes, peeled and cut in pieces
6 pork sausages, cut in pieces
2 cups rice
6 cups water
1 tablespoon chopped parsley
1 tablespoon chopped chives or green-onion tops
½ teaspoon pepper
   8 servings

Cut up the bacon in small pieces and put into a large, heavy frying pan. Add the cut-up chicken. Brown the chicken well, then add onion, salt, tomatoes, sausages, and rice. Fry for 10 minutes. Add water, parsley, chives, and pepper, and cook over medium heat until water is almost absorbed. The rice should be moist. Serve very hot.

141. RICE AND HAM (Arroz com Presunto)

   1 hour

1 tablespoon lard or vegetable fat
1 small onion, chopped
1 teaspoon garlic salt
4 tablespoons chopped parsley
4 tomatoes, peeled
2 cups rice
2 slices uncooked ham
4 cups water
4 hard-cooked eggs, sliced
olives
1 cup grated cheese
  6 servings

Make a *refogado* of the lard or fat, onion, garlic salt, parsley, and 2 of the tomatoes. Add the rice, ham cut in serving-size pieces, and water. Cook until rice is tender. Heap rice in the center of a hot platter, surround with pieces of ham, slices of hard-cooked egg, 2 tomatoes cut in slices, and olives. Sprinkle with grated cheese and serve very hot.

VEGETABLES

Vegetables in Brazil must be introduced by beans—black, all shades of brown, occasionally white, which, accompanied by rice, are the main article in the diet of the Brazilian. According to the income of the family, they assume a lesser or more important place, but they are available in every Brazilian home. They are cooked simply with some fat and seasonings, or are prepared as the traditional and famous *Feijoada à Brasileira*, (Recipe 142), which is served at festive luncheons, especially when there are foreign visitors. Delicious served with slices of orange and a small portion of *cachaça*, it is a dish for robust appetites.

Okra, summer squash, collards and other greens, potatoes, sweet and Irish, peas, and many more of the vegetables you know are commonly used. Squash and pumpkin are cooked as vegetables, and are also used to make a pretty yellow candy (Recipe 268). Green peppers are stuffed with a variety of combinations of meat, rice, onions, and cheese; and carrots in Brazil are as versatile a vegetable as they are in your country. Some of the recipes given are hearty enough to be used as a main dish for luncheon.

142. BRAZILIAN BLACK BEANS (Feijoada à Brasileira)

5 hours

2 pounds black beans
½ pound smoked tongue
1 pound smoked pork spareribs
1 pound smoked lean ham hocks
½ pound salt pork
salt
12 pork sausages, cut in pieces
2 tablespoons lard
1 large onion, grated
3 cloves garlic, minced
½ cup chopped parsley
10 servings

Pick over the beans, wash, and put to soak overnight in water. Put the smoked meats to soak overnight—in separate waters. In the morning, put the beans on to cook in the water in which they were soaked. Parboil the smoked meats and salt pork in fresh water. Remove skin from tongue. When beans are half cooked (about 2 hours), add parboiled meats and cook over low heat to avoid sticking. Add salt: the quantity depends on the salt in the smoked meats. Add water if necessary during cooking. When beans are almost tender, add cut-up pork sausages. Make a *refogado* of the lard, onion, garlic, and parsley. Cook lightly for a few minutes. When the beans are cooked and the meat is tender, add a cup of the beans to the *refogado* and mix well, return to bean pot, and taste for seasoning. Cook for about 10 minutes more. The beans should be thick but not soupy. Serve in large bowl or tureen, accompanied by Brazilian Rice (Recipe 138) and a plate of peeled, sliced oranges. If you like "hot" food, make a sauce of the juice of 3 lemons and mash in 6 small dried hot peppers. If you do not have a specialty store near you where you can buy the peppers, you may pick some of the dried red peppers out of the pickle spices.

143. EVERYDAY BEANS (Feijão Simples)

4 hours

2 pounds beans (may be black, brown, or pinto beans, or you may substitute kidney beans)
salt
1 thick slice salt pork
2 tablespoons lard
2 cloves garlic, minced
1 small onion, chopped
1 teaspoon pepper
8 servings

Soak the beans overnight. The next day, cook them in enough salted water to cover, with the salt pork. Separately make a *refogado* with lard, garlic, onion, and pepper. Add 1 cup of the beans, mix well, return to bean pot, and cook until beans are tender. Serve with Brazilian Rice (Recipe 138) and Farofa (Recipe 56).

144. TUTÚ OF BLACK BEANS *too-too'* (Tutú de Feijão Preto)

45 minutes

2 cups leftover seasoned black beans
meat stock (optional)
manioc flour or wheat flour
6 servings

Put the beans in the blender and grind until liquid. If there is no liquid with the beans, add a small amount of meat stock. Put on flame and heat, sift in enough manioc flour to thicken, or enough wheat flour (mixed with a little water), and cook for 10 minutes. The mixture should be the consistency of a very thick white sauce. Taste for seasoning. Spread on wide deep dish, and top with the following:

TOPPING

1 onion, cut in rings
2 tomatoes, peeled
2 tablespoons bacon fat or lard
salt
3 hard-cooked eggs, sliced

Cook the onion and tomatoes in the fat, adding salt, with care
not to break the onion rings. When onion and tomatoes are tender, spread mixture on top of the bean mixture, and top with
hard-cooked eggs. This dish is traditionally served with pork chops
or spareribs, along with Collards à Mineira (Recipe 161).

145. WHITE BEANS, MINAS STYLE (Feijão Branco à Moda de Minas)

4 hours

1 pound navy or white beans
½ pound smoked ham, raw
2 tablespoons chopped parsley
1 tablespoon chopped chives or green onion
1 tablespoon lard
1 clove garlic, minced
1 small onion, chopped
salt
½ teaspoon pepper
2 hard-cooked eggs, sliced
½ cup pitted green olives
croutons
   6 servings

Soak beans overnight, drain, and cook with smoked ham, parsley,
and chives, in enough water to cover until tender, adding water as
necessary. Make a *refogado* of the lard, garlic, onion, salt, and
pepper. Mix 1 cup cooked beans with the *refogado* and return to
the bean pot to cook. When tender, serve in individual bowls,
placing a slice of egg, 3 or 4 green olives, and croutons on top of
each.

146. STUFFED GREEN PEPPERS NO. 1
(Pimentão Recheado)

1½ hours

6 large green peppers
½ pound lean pork, chopped
1 cup cooked rice
1 teaspoon salt
2 tablespoons chopped ham
½ cup tomato sauce
½ cup hot water
1 pinch sugar
1 pinch pepper
  6 servings

Boil peppers 5 minutes, cut off tops, and remove seeds. Mix the chopped pork, rice, salt, and ham and fill the peppers. Mix the tomato sauce, water, pepper, and sugar. Set peppers in this mixture and cook, covered, over a low heat for 30 minutes. Remove to hot dish and pour sauce over peppers.

147. STUFFED GREEN PEPPERS NO. 2
(Pimentão Recheado)

1½ hours

4 large green peppers
2 tablespoons lard
1 medium-sized onion, chopped
½ cup bouillon
½ teaspoon salt
1 cup bread crumbs
½ cup milk
1 tablespoon chopped parsley
1 dash pepper
2 pork sausages, chopped and cooked
buttered crumbs
grated cheese
  4 servings

Cut peppers lengthwise, remove seeds, and cook in boiling water for 10 minutes. Make a *refogado* of lard and onion and add bouillon, salt, bread crumbs soaked in milk, parsley, pepper, and sausages. Stuff peppers with this mixture and sprinkle with buttered crumbs and grated cheese. Bake for 10 or 15 minutes in moderate oven, or until brown.

148. ANGÚ WITH VEGETABLES *ang-goo'* (Angú com Legumes)

2 hours

1 tablespoon lard
1 small onion, chopped
½ clove garlic, minced
1 tablespoon chopped parsley
1 teaspoon salt
1½ cups corn meal
3 cups milk
2 sweet potatoes, cooked and hot
3 Irish potatoes, cooked and hot
1 summer squash, cut in pieces, cooked and hot
3 carrots, cooked and hot
3 ears sweet corn, broken in two, cooked and hot
2 thick slices smoked ham, fried
6 to 8 servings

Make a *refogado* in a frying pan with the lard, onion, garlic, parsley, and salt. Mix the corn meal with the milk, so that there will be no lumps, add *refogado* and put on flame, stirring constantly; bring to boil and continue cooking until thick. Pile this *angú* in center of hot platter, surrounded by the hot cooked vegetables and hot fried ham, and pour over the corn-meal mixture, or *angú*, the following sauce:

SAUCE

2 tablespoons butter
1 large tomato, peeled and chopped
1 onion, chopped
1 tablespoon lemon juice
salt
½ cup water
¼ cup melted butter

Make a *refogado* of butter, tomato, and onion, and, when lightly cooked, add lemon juice, salt to taste, and water. Cook for 5 minutes and pour very hot over corn-meal mixture. Pour melted butter over the vegetables.

149. CARROT FAROFA *far-off'-ah* (Farofa de Cenouras)

½ hour

6 carrots
4 tablespoons butter or margarine
½ pound raisins
4 tablespoons manioc flour or dried bread crumbs
1 teaspoon salt
4 servings

Grate the carrots and fry in 2 tablespoons of the butter or margarine for 15 to 20 minutes. Stir in raisins, manioc flour or dried bread crumbs, the remaining tablespoons of butter, and salt. Stir together over flame for about 2 minutes. Serve very hot with baked, broiled, or fried meats.

150. FRIED ONIONS (Cebolas Fritas)

½ hour

3 large onions
2 eggs
2 tablespoons grated cheese
1 teaspoon salt
oil for frying
6 olives, stuffed
6 servings

Cut onions in slices. Beat eggs lightly and add grated cheese and salt. Dip onion slices in this mixture and fry in deep fat until golden brown. Serve on hot dish garnished with olives.

151. STUFFED ONIONS (Cebolas Recheadas)

1 hour 25 minutes
6 large onions
1 cup chopped shrimp, cooked and cleaned
2 tablespoons butter
flour
½ teaspoon salt
3 tomatoes
1 tablespoon white wine
½ cup water
1 tablespoon bread crumbs
2 tablespoons grated cheese
2 tablespoons melted butter
6 servings

Peel and cook onions in salted water until tender. Drain. Make cavity in each onion for the stuffing, reserving pulp. Fill onion with chopped shrimp. Chop pulp that was taken from the onions and fry in butter, sprinkle with about 1 tablespoon flour, salt, and brown well. Add tomatoes, wine, and water and cook a few minutes until thick. Put the stuffed onions in a baking dish and cover with sauce, topping with bread crumbs, grated cheese, and melted butter. Brown in oven for about 10 minutes.

152. CABBAGE MOLD (Bôlo de Repôlho)

1 hour
1 medium-sized head cabbage
3 eggs, beaten
1 tablespoon melted butter
1 tablespoon flour
1 cup milk
¾ teaspoon salt
4 to 6 servings

Cut cabbage in fine shreds and cook in salted water for 15 minutes. Drain and cool. Mix eggs, butter, flour, milk, and salt with cabbage. Bake in a buttered baking pan for about ½ hour at 400 degrees, or until custard is set.

153. STUFFED CABBAGE (Repôlho Recheado)

1½ hours

1 large cabbage
3 teaspoons salt
2 tablespoons butter
2 small onions
1 clove garlic, minced
½ pound beef, ground
2 small tomatoes, peeled and chopped
1 dash pepper
½ cup water
1 tablespoon flour
2 tablespoons grated cheese
6 servings

Separate and wash each leaf of cabbage carefully, and cook in water with 1 teaspoon salt. Make a *refogado* of 2 tablespoons butter, 1 onion chopped, garlic, and 1 teaspoon salt. Add the ground beef and cook for 5 minutes. Place spoons of this mixture in center of each leaf, roll up, and tie with a string or fasten with toothpicks. Simmer 35 to 40 minutes in a sauce made of the other onion, chopped, the tomatoes, 1 teaspoon salt, pepper, and ½ cup water. When cooked, remove from sauce, remove thread or toothpicks carefully, and thicken the sauce with flour. Pour over the stuffed cabbage leaves and sprinkle with grated cheese.

154. CAULIFLOWER PIE (Torta de Couve-Flor)

1 hour

1 large cauliflower
salt
2 tablespoons butter
2 tablespoons flour
1 dash nutmeg
½ cup cream
2 egg yolks
4 tablespoons grated Parmesan cheese
melted butter
   6 servings

Separate flowers and boil until tender in salted water, but do not overcook. Brown butter and flour, pour in 1½ cups of the water in which you cooked the cauliflower, and add the nutmeg. Cook until it thickens. Beat cream and egg yolks together and add to the sauce. Taste for salt. Place the cauliflower in a buttered casserole, cover with sauce, grated cheese, and melted butter, put into a moderate oven, and bake until it bubbles and cheese is melted.

155. CAULIFLOWER CASSEROLE (Couve-Flor de Panela)

1 hour

3 carrots, scraped and sliced
3 potatoes, peeled and sliced
1 tablespoon lard
1 small onion, chopped
½ teaspoon salt
1 tablespoon parsley
1 large onion, sliced
3 tomatoes, peeled and sliced
1 cauliflower
4 slices bacon
   4 to 6 servings

Cook carrots and potatoes slightly in salted water. In a heavy saucepan, make a *refogado* of lard, chopped onion, salt, and parsley. Place on this a layer of sliced potatoes, then the carrots, then the sliced onion, then the sliced tomatoes, sprinkle with salt, and put the cauliflower, which has been broken into flowers, on top of all. Cover with the bacon slices, cover tightly, and cook over very low heat until cauliflower is done.

156. BAKED EGGPLANT (Beringela ao Fôrno)

1 hour

1 eggplant
4 tablespoons chopped mushrooms
2 tablespoons butter
½ teaspoon salt
1 dash pepper
½ tablespoon parsley
½ pound chopped ham
3 hard-cooked eggs, chopped
8 anchovies, cut in pieces
6 servings

Cook eggplant in salted water for 10 minutes, cut off top, and remove pulp, leaving enough for a shell. Reserve pulp. In a saucepan, fry mushrooms in butter, add salt, pepper, and parsley. Cool. Add this to the eggplant pulp, chopped, with ham, chopped eggs, and cut-up anchovies. Fill eggplant shell with this mixture and bake in a 350-degree oven about ½ hour, or until eggplant is tender.

157. CHAYOTE PUDDING (Bôlo de Chuchu)

50 minutes

3 chayotes, peeled, cored, and cut in pieces
½ cup milk
3 eggs, beaten
½ teaspoon salt
3 tablespoons grated cheese
2 tablespoons melted butter
2 tablespoons flour
2 hard-cooked eggs, sliced
chives, chopped
6 servings

Cook chayotes in small amount of salted water, drain, and press through a sieve. (Be careful not to cook them too long or they lose their green color.) Combine milk, eggs, salt, grated cheese, melted butter, and flour, and mix with chayotes. Bake in buttered dish for about 20 minutes at 375 degrees, or until set. Garnish with slices of hard-cooked eggs and chopped chives.

158. CARROT PUDDING (Pudim de Cenouras)

1½ hours

1 pound carrots
5 eggs
1 teaspoon salt
1 teaspoon sugar
½ teaspoon grated lemon rind
1½ cups soft bread crumbs
2 tablespoons melted butter
   4 to 6 servings

Scrape and grind carrots in the blender. Beat egg whites stiff, fold in beaten yolks, and salt, sugar, lemon rind, 1 cup bread crumbs, melted butter, and carrots. Grease and crumb the bottom and sides of a double boiler and pour in carrot mixture. Cook for 1 hour over hot water. Unmold on hot dish and serve with mixed green salad.

159. SPINACH MOLDS (Espinafre em Forminhas)

1½ hours

1½ cups cooked, drained spinach
2 tablespoons flour
2 tablespoons butter
1 cup beef bouillon
1 teaspoon salt
1 dash pepper
2 whole eggs
3 egg yolks
6 slices cooked ham
2 hard-cooked eggs, sliced
   6 servings

Press the spinach through a sieve. Brown the flour in the butter and add the bouillon and spinach and cook, stirring constantly until thick. Remove from flame and add salt and pepper. Cool, and mix in the whole eggs and egg yolks beaten together. Put mixture in 6 small buttered molds and bake in pan containing hot water for 20 minutes, or until well set. Fry ham lightly in a little butter, and serve each mold turned over a slice of ham, garnished with hard-cooked eggs.

160. SPINACH PUDDING (Pudim de Espinafre)

A complete and delicious meal for a meatless day.

> 1½ hours
> 2 tablespoons grated onion
> 1 tablespoon butter or margarine
> 2 cups spinach, cooked
> 4 slices white bread, cut in pieces
> 5 egg yolks
> 1 tablespoon melted butter
> 1 dash nutmeg
> 1 teaspoon salt
> 1 dash pepper
> bread crumbs
>   6 servings

Brown onion in 1 tablespoon butter or margarine. Add spinach and cut-up bread and grind. Beat egg yolks and 1 tablespoon melted butter until creamy, add nutmeg, salt, and pepper and combine with the spinach mixture. Butter top of double boiler and sprinkle with dry bread crumbs. Fill with spinach mixture and cook over water for 1 hour. Unmold and serve with following sauce:

SAUCE

> 4 tablespoons butter
> 4 tablespoons flour
> 2 cups hot milk
> 2 egg yolks, beaten
> 1 teaspoon salt
> 1 dash pepper

Melt butter and mix in flour, add hot milk, and beat fast to avoid lumps. Return to stove, cook, stirring constantly, until creamy. Remove from flame, add beaten egg yolks, salt, and pepper. Pour over spinach mold.

161. COLLARDS À MINEIRA (Couve à Mineira)

20 minutes

collard greens
lard or drippings
salt

Wash the collard leaves, put 3 or 4 together, and roll into tight roll, then shred as finely as possible (like cabbage for salad). For every cup of shredded collard, use 1 tablespoon of lard or drippings. Heat fat in heavy pan, put in greens, and toss until hot and well mixed with the fat. Shake in salt to taste. Serve hot.

CAKES and COOKIES

Cakes for tea or afternoon coffee are usually unfrosted, quite sweet, with fruit, coconut, or nuts. Some of these sweet cakes could be served with whipped cream as a dessert. Try the Orange Cake (Recipe 166), warm with cream one day, and cold the next day, with coffee or for a school lunch. It will be just as delicious—it seems to get better every day. Brazil-nut Wine Cake (Recipe 168) and the Prune-filled Almond Cake (Recipe 169) are those "something different" recipes that you have been looking for. For a genuine Brazilian touch at your next tea party, have a plate of Quindins (Recipe 176) or the delicious Filled Coconut and Pineapple Squares (Recipe 183). Included in this chapter is Cuscuz (Recipe 162). It is not exactly a cake, but it is served at teatime and goes very well with a cup of hot Coffee with Milk (Recipe 278).

162. Cuscuz (koos-koos')

½ hour

2 cups boiling water
2 cups minute tapioca
½ teaspoon salt
1½ cups sugar
2 cups grated coconut, preferably fresh
¾ cup coconut milk
10 servings

Pour the boiling water over the tapioca, salt, sugar, and half the grated coconut and mix well. Pour mixture into an 8-inch round mold—the mixture should be about 3 inches in depth. Cover mold, wrap in cloth, and put in the refrigerator until the next day. Turn mold onto deep plate, pour over it the coconut milk, and sprinkle with the rest of the grated coconut. Cut in wedges to serve.

163. Pineapple Cake (Bôlo de Abacaxi)

1½ hours

3 tablespoons sugar
2 tablespoons butter
1 fresh pineapple
6 prunes, cooked and pitted
3 eggs
2 cups sugar
1 cup milk
1½ cups cake flour
1 teaspoon baking powder
8 servings

Melt the 3 tablespoons sugar and 1 tablespoon butter in the baking pan and stir over the flame until golden brown. Tilt pan so the syrup will coat the sides as well as the bottom. Wash and peel the pineapple, cut in slices, and remove core. Save the peel. Cook the pineapple in a very small amount of water for 15 minutes. Arrange the slices on the bottom of the baking pan, with a prune in the center of each. Beat egg yolks until thick, add 1 cup sugar, milk, and flour sifted with baking powder. Fold in stiffly beaten egg whites. Pour in the pan over the pineapple slices and bake for about 40 minutes at 375 degrees. Turn the pan upside down on a large plate to remove the cake. Pour over it the following syrup: boil the pineapple peel in water, strain, and add the other cup sugar and the remaining tablespoon butter. Cook until thick. The cooking water from the pineapple slices may be used in this syrup (there should be about 1½ cups).

164. MARILÚ'S CAKE SQUARES (Bôlo Marilú)

  1 hour

  5 tablespoons sugar
  1½ tablespoons butter
  3 eggs
  6 tablespoons flour
  1 teaspoon baking powder
  ½ teaspoon vanilla
  12 squares

Beat sugar and butter until creamy. Add egg yolks and sifted flour mixed with baking powder. Add vanilla. Mix thoroughly and fold in beaten egg whites. Pour into a buttered square baking pan to about ½-inch thickness and bake for ½ hour, at 375 degrees. Cover with the following frosting:

FROSTING

  1 egg white
  ½ cup sugar
  1 teaspoon cocoa

Beat egg white and add sugar and cocoa, mixing well. Spread over cake while still hot. Cool and cut into small squares.

165. BEER CAKE (Bôlo de Cerveja)

  1½ hours

  3 cups sugar
  6 tablespoons butter
  6 eggs
  3 cups sifted flour
  1½ cups bock beer
  15 servings

Beat sugar and butter until creamy, add egg yolks, and beat well. Add flour and beer alternately and beat. Fold in stiffly beaten egg whites. Pour into a greased, floured 9-inch round loaf pan and bake for 1 hour in a 375-degree oven.

166. ORANGE CAKE (Bôlo de Laranja)

1 hour 15 minutes
½ cup butter
2½ cups sugar
1 orange
3 eggs
¼ teaspoon salt
½ teaspoon baking soda
1 teaspoon baking powder
2 cups cake flour
½ cup milk
1 cup orange juice
whipped cream (optional)
12 servings

Beat butter and 2 cups sugar until creamy, add grated orange rind, egg yolks, and salt, and beat again. Add the juice of the orange. Sift the baking soda, baking powder, and flour together and add alternately with the milk. Last, add the beaten egg whites. Put in a greased and floured 9-inch square pan. Bake for 40 minutes at 375 degrees. While cake is still hot, pour over it the following: 1 cup orange juice mixed with ½ cup sugar. Let cake cool before serving. May be served with whipped cream.

167. BAHIA COCONUT CAKE (Bôlo Baiano)

1 hour 15 minutes
8 tablespoons butter
1½ cups sugar
6 eggs
1 fresh coconut, grated, or 1 cup shredded coconut soaked in ⅓ cup coconut milk for 15 minutes
1½ cups flour
10 servings

Beat butter and sugar until creamy, add egg yolks, and continue beating. Mix in the fresh or the shredded coconut. Add flour and beat well. Fold in stiffly beaten egg whites. Pour into a deep, round greased and floured 9-inch baking pan and bake 40 minutes at 375 degrees, or until cake is done.

168. BRAZIL-NUT WINE CAKE (Bôlo de Nozes com Vinho)

> 1½ hours

1 cup butter
4 cups sugar
12 egg yolks, beaten
4 cups sifted flour
3 teaspoons baking powder
½ teaspoon salt
2 teaspoons cocoa
1 teaspoon cinnamon
2 cups milk
½ cup port wine
2 cups finely chopped Brazil nuts
6 egg whites
20 servings

Beat butter and sugar until creamy, add egg yolks, and beat well. Sift flour, baking powder, salt, cocoa, and cinnamon together. Add to first mixture alternately with milk and wine and stir in the chopped nuts. Fold in the beaten egg whites. Bake in greased and floured tube pan, 10 inches in diameter and 4 inches high, for 1 hour at 375 degrees.

169. PRUNE-FILLED ALMOND CAKE (Bôlo Recheado de Ameixas)

   1 hour 15 minutes
   1 cup butter
   2 cups sugar
   6 eggs
   2 cups flour
   1 teaspoon baking powder
   2 tablespoons cocoa
   1 cup chopped almonds
   1 cup prune preserve
   powdered sugar
      12 servings

Beat butter and sugar until creamy, add eggs, one at a time, beating for 15 minutes by hand, or 5 minutes with an electric beater. Add flour sifted with baking powder and beat again. Divide batter into 2 parts; add the cocoa to one and the chopped almonds to the other. Pour batter into two 9-inch layer-cake pans, which have been greased and floured. Bake in a 375-degree oven for about ½ hour. Cool and remove from pan and put together with the prune preserve as filling. Dust powdered sugar over the top.

170. WONDER CAKE (Bôlo Maioral)

   1½ hours
   2 cups butter
   3 cups sugar
   8 eggs
   3 cups flour
   1 teaspoon baking powder
   ½ cup milk
   5 slices canned pineapple, or 3 apples, peeled and sliced
   1 cup sugar
      15 servings

Beat butter and 2 cups of sugar until creamy. Add egg yolks, one at a time, beating thoroughly; add the flour and baking powder sifted together alternately with the milk. Melt the last cup of sugar in the baking pan until golden brown and let cool. Place the pineapple slices or apple slices on bottom of baking pan over the syrup and pour batter over them. Bake for 1 hour at 375 degrees.

171. GOLDEN CAKE (Bôlo de Ouro)

1 hour 15 minutes
½ cup butter
1 cup sugar
8 egg yolks, beaten
½ cup milk
1¾ cups cake flour
3 teaspoons baking powder
1 teaspoon vanilla
10 servings

Beat butter and sugar until creamy, add beaten yolks, stir in milk, and the flour and baking powder sifted together. Add vanilla. Pour mixture in deep 9-inch buttered and floured baking pan and bake for 35 to 40 minutes at 350 degrees, or until done.

172. CORNSTARCH BUTTER COOKIES (Biscoitos de Maizena)

These crumbly, delicate brown tidbits are the cookies most commonly eaten in all Brazilian homes. Bake some and you will see why.

1½ hours
1 cup butter
1 cup sugar
1 cup cake flour
2 cups cornstarch
100 very small cookies

Cream butter and sugar, work in the flour and cornstarch, which have been sifted together. Roll or pat out on floured board to about ⅜-inch thickness. Cut cookies 1 inch in diameter. Put on cooky sheet. Bake ½ hour in a 300-degree oven.

173. BRAZIL-NUT SANDWICHES (Docinhos do Pará)

1 hour 15 minutes

6 tablespoons butter
4 tablespoons sugar
6 tablespoons cornstarch
6 tablespoons flour
6 tablespoons ground Brazil nuts
jelly
About 12 sandwiches

Mix butter and sugar until creamy, work in the dry ingredients sifted together and the nuts. Roll out on floured board to ¼-inch thickness and cut with 2-inch cooky cutter. Bake in a 350-degree oven about 20 minutes, or until very light brown. Cool and put cookies together with jelly, making little sandwiches.

174. BRAZILIAN BROWNIES (Pedacinhos de Chocolate)

1 hour

2 tablespoons butter
4 tablespoons sugar
3 eggs
4 tablespoons flour
1 teaspoon baking powder
3 tablespoons cocoa
1 tablespoon white wine
About 18 brownies

Mix butter and sugar until creamy, add eggs, and flour, baking powder, and cocoa sifted together. Mix well and add wine. Turn into an 8-inch greased baking pan and bake for 25 minutes at 350 degrees. Cut into small squares while still hot.

175. Coconut Bars (Fatias de Côco)

1 hour

2 cups sugar
4 egg yolks, beaten
1 cup shredded coconut
½ cup grated American cheese
sugar
cinnamon
   About 12 bars

Beat the sugar in the egg yolks, add coconut and grated cheese. Turn into 8-inch-square baking pan, which has been greased and dusted with flour. Bake for about ½ hour at 325 degrees. When slightly cool, cut into small bars, and roll in a mixture of sugar and cinnamon.

Quindins are a typical Brazilian sweet, almost a candy, but served with afternoon tea as a small cake. The secret of a perfect *quindim* is in the baking: the top should be delicately browned and the bottom, when turned over on a plate, should be a tender jelly. The first time you make them, turn one out to see if it is of the right consistency before you remove them all from the oven. Remember that they should be small; if molds or muffin tins are large, use less "dough"—about 1 inch in the bottom of the mold would be right. Put the filled molds in a shallow pan containing 1 inch of hot water and bake for 45 to 50 minutes at 350 degrees. Choose one of the following variations. Don't forget to put them upside down in white paper cups to serve. They will look like daisies on a pretty plate.

176. QUINDINS (*keen-deens'*)

> 1 hour 15 minutes

> 2 cups sugar
> 2 tablespoons melted butter
> 18 egg yolks
> 1 cup shredded coconut
>> 18 to 30 cakes, depending on size

Stir all ingredients together and mix well. Put in greased molds and bake according to directions above.

177. QUINDINS WITH COCONUT MILK (Quindins com Leite de Côco)

> 1 hour 15 minutes

> 2 cups sugar
> 1 tablespoon melted butter
> 12 egg yolks
> ¾ cup coconut milk
>> About 20 cakes

Proceed as in Recipe 176.

178. QUINDINS WITH RAISINS (Quindins com Passas)

> 1 hour 15 minutes

> 2 cups sugar
> ¾ cup water
> 2 tablespoons butter
> 24 egg yolks
> ¾ cup coconut milk
> raisins, washed
>> 24 to 40 cakes, depending on size

Make a syrup of sugar and water according to Recipe 244. Stir butter into syrup and cool. Stir in egg yolks and coconut milk and mix well. Put two raisins in each greased mold, and spoon mixture into molds. Bake according to directions above.

156

179. DELICATE QUINDINS (Delícias de Côco)

> 1 hour 15 minutes

- 12 egg yolks
- 1 egg white
- 2 cups sugar
- 2 cups shredded coconut
- 2 tablespoons melted butter
  About 12 to 20 cakes

Combine all ingredients and mix well. Bake according to directions above.

180. QUINDINS WITH CHEESE (Quindins com Queijo)

> 1 hour 15 minutes

- 1 cup sugar
- ½ cup water
- ¼ cup butter
- 2 tablespoons grated cheese
- 6 egg yolks
  About 8 to 16 cakes

Make a syrup of sugar and water according to Recipe 244. Add butter. Cool. Mix cheese and egg yolks and add to syrup, stirring well but not beating. Bake according to directions above.

181. MOTHER BENTA'S CUPCAKES NO. 1
(Mãe Benta No. 1)

   1 hour

   2 cups butter
   2 cups sugar
   9 eggs
   2 cups rice flour
   1 cup shredded coconut
   3 tablespoons grated fresh coconut
   ½ cup coconut milk
   1 teaspoon baking powder
   About 36 cakes

Beat butter and sugar until creamy and add egg yolks, one at a
time, beating after each addition. Mix in rice flour, add shredded
coconut, and mix well. Finally fold in stiffly beaten egg whites and
the fresh coconut, coconut milk and baking powder, previously
mixed. Spoon dough into small greased cupcake molds or fluted
paper cups ⅔ full and bake for about 20 minutes in a 325-degree
oven, or until golden brown.

182. MOTHER BENTA'S CUPCAKES NO. 2
(Mãe Benta No. 2)

   1 hour

   6 egg yolks
   1 egg white
   1 cup sugar
   1 medium-sized potato, freshly boiled and mashed
   4 tablespoons melted butter
   5 tablespoons shredded coconut
   1 cup rice flour
   4 tablespoons cold water
   About 18 cupcakes

Beat egg yolks and egg white well, add sugar, mashed potato,
melted butter, coconut, and rice flour. Mix in cold water last. Put
in fluted paper cups, using about 2 tablespoons of the dough for each
cup. Bake for about 20 minutes at 325 degrees, or until golden
brown.

183. FILLED COCONUT AND PINEAPPLE SQUARES (Quadradinhos)

1½ hours

1 cup butter
3 cups sugar
3 eggs
3 cups flour
1 teaspoon baking powder
salt
1 egg yolk
crystallized sugar
   24 squares

Beat sugar and butter together, beat in eggs, and work in the flour, sifted with baking powder and salt. Divide in two parts. Roll out one part so that it lines a large square or oblong baking pan, pour in the filling, and cover with other half of dough, brush with egg yolk, and bake for about ½ hour at 350 degrees, or until brown. Sprinkle with crystallized sugar. Cut into squares.

FILLING

1½ cups shredded coconut
1 pineapple, crushed
4 cups sugar
2 tablespoons butter

Mix all ingredients and cook, stirring constantly until it pulls away from side of pan. Cool.

184. NEWLYWEDS (Casadinhos)

1 hour

¾ cup sugar
½ cup butter
1¾ cups flour
strawberry jam
confectioners' sugar
   18 cookies

Beat butter and sugar until creamy, work in flour. Pat out on a board until about ½ inch in thickness. Cut with small cutter, not over 1½ inches, put on baking sheet, and bake at 350 degrees for 10 or 15 minutes, or until golden brown. Remove from oven, cool. Put two together with strawberry jam and roll in confectioners' sugar. You may use Recipe 217 or 264 for the filling if you wish.

185. SPONGE CAKES WITH RUM (Docinhos Estufados)
40 minutes

3 eggs
5 tablespoons sugar
5 tablespoons potato flour
rum
  About 12 cakes

Beat egg whites until stiff, add unbeaten yolks, fold in sugar and potato flour sifted together. Pour into small greased and floured muffin tins and bake for about 20 minutes at 350 degrees, or until golden brown. While still hot, dip a teaspoon of rum over each one.

186. HURRY! HURRY! (Corre-Corre)
½ hour

2 eggs
4 tablespoons melted butter
1 cup sugar
1 cup rice flour
  About 12 cakes

Beat eggs, mix in sugar and melted butter and, last, the rice flour. Pour into greased and floured muffin tins, and bake for about 20 minutes at 350 degrees, or until golden brown. Serve with chocolate ice cream.

187. CABOCLA'S KISSES (Beijinhos de Cabocla)

45 minutes

3 eggs
3 tablespoons melted butter
¾ cup sugar
6 tablespoons flour
1 coconut, grated
powdered sugar
18 cakes

Beat the egg whites stiff, add the yolks, the butter, and the sugar and flour sifted together. Add coconut. Put in greased muffin tins or fluted paper cups to bake. Bake about 15 minutes in a 350-degree oven, or until light brown. Sprinkle with powdered sugar.

188. BRAZIL-NUT MACAROONS (Doces de Castanha do Pará)

1 hour 45 minutes

1½ cups ground Brazil nuts
¾ cup sugar
3 egg whites
18 macaroons

Mix the 3 ingredients and cook, stirring constantly, until you can see bottom of the pan. Drop by teaspoons on greased, floured cooky sheet. Let stand 1 hour. Bake 25 minutes at 300 degrees, being very careful not to burn.

NOTE: See also Recipe 283 for COFFEE CAKE.

DESSERTS

Brazilians serve custards and many concoctions of corn, corn meal, and hominy as desserts, as well as gelatins and fruit. The rich custards are combinations of eggs, milk, orange juice, or coconut milk, flavored with coffee, caramel, or nuts. Guava or other fruit pastes served with cheese is on the menu any day of the year. Guava paste can be obtained at specialty food stores, but if not available, serve fruit or jam with your favorite cheese to finish off a Brazilian-style dinner. Avocado Cream (Recipe 235) served ice-cold in clear glass dishes is light, easy to prepare, and delightful to look at. Bananas are served plain or cooked in various ways, and oranges, peeled with a knife, so that none of the white skin remains, are brought to the table and are eaten with knife and fork. Fruit salad served icy cold is a Brazilian favorite, and simple to prepare.

The caramelized sugar used to line the dishes for baking various custards and puddings is made by melting the sugar over a low flame in a heavy pan, stirring constantly, then pouring the syrup into a baking dish which has been warmed (so the syrup will not harden quickly), and tilting the dish so that the bottom and the sides are coated. Or the sugar can be melted in the baking dish if it is of aluminum or other flame-resistant material. The texture of these custards should be smooth and velvety. Be careful not to overbake. Insert a knife in the center, and if it comes out clean, the custard is done.

189. Ambrosia (ahm-bro'-zee-ah)

45 minutes

4 cups sugar
1½ cups water
12 egg yolks
6 egg whites
4 cups milk
1 teaspoon cinnamon
6 whole cloves
12 servings

Make syrup of sugar and water, cooking until it spins a thread.
Cool. Beat yolks and whites slightly, mix with milk, and strain
through wire sieve. Mix with syrup. Bring to a boil over low heat
without stirring. Cook until golden in color, stirring now and then,
add cinnamon and cloves. Serve cold.

190. Corn and Coconut Pudding (Tigelinhas de Milho Verde) from Recife

1 hour 15 minutes

3 tablespoons cornstarch
2 cups milk
4 egg yolks, beaten
½ teaspoon salt
2 cups sugar
¾ cup coconut milk
2 cups cream-style corn
1 tablespoon melted butter
½ teaspoon anise extract
10 servings

Cook the cornstarch and milk over a low flame until it thickens.
Cool. Mix in egg yolks and all other ingredients and pour into buttered custard cups. Bake for 25 to 30 minutes in pan containing 1
inch of hot water, until set.

191. GREEN-CORN CANJIQUINHA *can-gee-keen'-ya* (Canjiquinha de Milho Verde)

1 hour

1 10-ounce package of frozen corn or an equal quantity of fresh
  corn cut from cob
2 tablespoons cornstarch
1½ cups coconut milk
1½ cups sugar
½ teaspoon anise extract
  8 servings

Cook and grind the corn. Mix the cornstarch with coconut milk
and put in a double boiler to thicken. Mix the sugar and corn into
the coconut-milk cream and add anise extract. Cook a few minutes
more. Turn into pudding dish. Serve cold.

192. FINE CORN-MEAL PUDDING (Creme de Fubarina)

1 hour 15 minutes

3 cups milk
2 teaspoons butter
½ teaspoon salt
6 tablespoons sugar
½ cup finest corn meal
¾ cup coconut milk
4 eggs, beaten
1 teaspoon vanilla
2 tablespoons cottage cheese
  8 servings

Heat milk, butter, salt, and sugar in the top of a double boiler,
and sift in the corn meal, or mix it with a small amount of water and
then add. Cook to a smooth gruel. Cool. Add coconut milk, beaten
eggs, vanilla, and cottage cheese. Mix and turn into greased pudding
dish and bake for 40 minutes at 375 degrees, or until set.

193. HEAVENLY CARAMEL CUSTARD (Creme Queimado do Céu)

1 hour

½ cup sugar for caramel
6 egg yolks
6 tablespoons sugar
1 cup milk
1 teaspoon vanilla
  6 servings

Melt the ½ cup sugar in a small ring mold over a low flame, tilting the pan so that the caramel coats the sides well. Beat egg yolks slightly, mix in sugar, add milk and vanilla, mix well, and pour into mold. Put in pan containing 1 inch of hot water and bake about 40 minutes at 375 degrees. Test with knife to see if it is done. When cool, turn out on a deep plate. The caramel will make a sauce over the pudding.

194. VELVET CUSTARD (Creme Veludo)

1 hour

1 can sweetened condensed milk
1 can milk (measured in condensed-milk can)
4 eggs
½ cup sugar
  4 servings

Put first three ingredients in bowl and beat well. Pour into pan lined with ½ cup caramelized sugar and bake in a 375-degree oven in pan containing 1 inch of hot water for about 40 minutes. Test with knife to see if it is done. Unmold on deep plate when cool.

195. ORANGE CUSTARD (Creme de Laranja)

1 hour

1 tablespoon cornstarch
½ cup orange juice
juice of ½ lemon
1¼ cups sugar
1½ tablespoons butter
5 eggs, beaten
6 servings

Cook the cornstarch in a double boiler with the orange and lemon juice. Add ¾ cup sugar. Add butter and cool. Add the beaten eggs. Turn into mold lined with ½ cup caramelized sugar. Bake in pan containing 1 inch of hot water for about 40 minutes at 375 degrees. Test with knife to see if it is done. When cool, unmold on deep plate.

196. MARY'S CUSTARD (Pudim Mary)

1 hour

3 eggs
1 cup orange juice
1 can sweetened condensed milk
½ cup sugar
4 servings

Beat yolks, add orange juice and condensed milk. Fold in well-beaten egg whites. Pour into mold lined with ½ cup caramelized sugar. Bake in pan containing 1 inch of hot water for 40 minutes at 375 degrees. Test with knife to see if it is done. When cool, unmold on deep plate.

197. ORANGE CUSTARD CUPS (Copinhos de Laranja)

1 hour

2 cups sugar
10 eggs
2 tablespoons milk
1 cup orange juice
  6 servings

Beat sugar, egg yolks, milk, and orange juice together. Fold in stiffly beaten egg whites and pour into individual greased custard cups. Bake for about 25 minutes in a pan containing 1 inch of water at 375 degrees.

198. PARADISE PUDDING (Pudim Paraiso)

1½ hours

4½ cups sugar
1½ cups water
1 teaspoon vanilla
12 egg yolks
1 egg white
2 cups ground almonds
2 tablespoons melted butter
  8 servings

Make a syrup of 4 cups sugar and the water, according to Recipe 244. Cool. Add vanilla, egg yolks and egg white beaten together, almonds, and butter. Mix well and pour into a mold lined with ½ cup caramelized sugar and bake for 40 minutes in a pan containing 1 inch of water at 375 degrees. When cool, unmold on deep plate. Serve warm or cold.

199. PRUNE CUSTARD (Pudim de Ameixas)

1½ hours

2 cups milk
1 cup sugar
2 tablespoons cornstarch
¼ teaspoon salt
1 cup mashed, cooked, unsweetened prunes
6 egg yolks
3 egg whites
½ teaspoon cinnamon
8 servings

Heat the milk, add sugar and cornstarch and salt. Cook until thick. While still hot, add the prunes and cool. Add beaten egg yolks, beaten whites, and cinnamon. Pour into greased mold and bake in a pan containing 1 inch of water at 375 degrees for 40 minutes, or until set. Unmold when cool.

200. MARVELOUS CHEESE CUSTARD (Pudim Maravilhoso)

1½ hours

2 cups sugar
¾ cup water
2 tablespoons melted butter
¾ cup coconut milk
6 eggs, beaten
1 cup grated American cheese
6 servings

Make a syrup of the sugar and water, according to Recipe 244. Cool and add the melted butter, coconut milk, eggs, and grated cheese. Pour into buttered mold and bake in a pan containing 1 inch of hot water for 40 minutes at 375 degrees. Test with knife. When cool, unmold on deep plate.

201. LEMON CUSTARD (Pudim de Leite com Limão)

1½ hours

12 egg yolks
4 egg whites
4 cups sugar
2 cups milk
1 tablespoon lemon juice
grated rind of 1 lemon
½ cup sugar
8 servings

Beat egg yolks and whites and sugar until creamy. Add milk and strain through a sieve. Add lemon juice and rind and pour into a mold lined with caramelized sugar. Place in baking pan containing 1 inch of hot water and bake for 40 to 50 minutes at 375 degrees, or until set. When cool, unmold on deep plate.

202. CHEESE CUP CUSTARD (Pudimzinho de Queijo)

1 hour

3 tablespoons butter
3 cups sugar
8 egg yolks
5 tablespoons flour
5 tablespoons grated American cream cheese
4 egg whites, beaten
6 to 8 servings

Cream butter and sugar, add egg yolks one at a time, add flour and cheese, and, last, the egg whites. Turn into greased custard cups, and bake for 35 to 40 minutes at 375 degrees in pan containing 1 inch of hot water.

203. ORANGE DELIGHT CUSTARD (Bom Bocado de Laranja)

> 1 hour 15 minutes

3 cups sugar
1¼ cups water
2 teaspoons butter
1½ cups orange juice
3 tablespoons flour
5 egg yolks
2 egg whites
8 to 10 prunes, cooked and pitted (optional)
> 8 to 10 servings

Make a syrup of sugar and water, according to Recipe 244, adding the butter while cooking. Cool and add 1 cup orange juice; mix the remaining ½ cup with the flour to a smooth paste; add to syrup. Beat eggs yolks and whites slightly, add to first mixture, and strain several times. Pour into greased custard cups, set in a pan containing 1 inch of hot water, and bake for ½ hour at 375 degrees, or until set. You may put a pitted cooked prune in the bottom of each custard cup before pouring in the mixture, if you wish.

204. CRUMB PUDDING (Pudim de Biscoito)

> 1 hour 15 minutes

3 cups sugar
1¼ cups water
12 egg yolks
1 cup vanilla-wafer or graham-cracker crumbs
2 tablespoons melted butter
1½ cups grated American cheese
6 egg whites
> 8 servings

Make a syrup of sugar and water, according to Recipe 244, cool, and add egg yolks, crumbs, melted butter, cheese, and stiffly beaten egg whites. Mix well and pour into buttered mold, and bake for 40 minutes in a 375-degree oven in a baking pan containing 1 inch of hot water. Cool and turn out on deep plate.

205. MOTHER'S COCONUT PUDDING (Pudim da Velha)

1½ hours

3 cups sugar
1¼ cups water
1 cup grated American cheese
1 tablespoon melted butter
2 slices white bread
1 fresh coconut, grated, or 1½ cups shredded coconut
½ teaspoon cinnamon
5 eggs
8 servings

Make a syrup of sugar and water, according to Recipe 244. Mix the cheese, melted butter, crumbs pulled from the 2 slices of bread, coconut, and cinnamon and add to syrup. Beat eggs and fold into the mixture. Bake in a buttered loaf pan for 40 minutes at 375 degrees, or until firm.

206. EASY FRUIT PUDDING (Pudim Ligeiro)

3 hours

buttered slices of white bread (about 3)
½ cup raisins
1 cup mixed candied peel (citron, orange, lemon)
½ cup pitted dates
2 tablespoons jelly
3 cups milk
2 tablespoons cornstarch
3 egg yolks
1 cup sugar
8 servings

Arrange the slices of buttered bread in the bottom of a greased baking dish, dot with raisins, candied peel, dates, and jelly. Make a cream of the milk, cornstarch, egg yolks, and sugar. Pour this over the bread and fruits, let stand for 2 hours, then bake for about ½ hour in a 400-degree oven. Serve warm or cold.

207. BREAD PUDDING (Pudim de Pão)

1½ hours

4 cups milk
6 slices white bread
4 tablespoons butter
3 tablespoons grated American cheese
¼ teaspoon nutmeg
½ teaspoon cloves
½ teaspoon cinnamon
2 cups sugar
12 egg yolks, beaten
½ cup seedless raisins
½ cup mixed candied peel (citron, orange, lemon)
5 egg whites
whipped cream
12 servings

Heat milk, remove crusts from bread and crumble soft part into the hot milk. Stir in the butter, cheese, nutmeg, cloves, cinnamon, sugar, egg yolks, raisins, and chopped peel. Fold in stiffly beaten egg whites. Pour into buttered mold and bake for 40 minutes in a 375-degree oven, or until firm. Unmold on deep plate and serve warm or cold with whipped cream.

208. COCONUT BREAD PUDDING (Pudim de Pão com Côco)

1½ hours

4 slices white bread
2 cups milk
1 cup sugar
¾ cup coconut milk
2 teaspoons melted butter
1 cup shredded coconut
6 egg yolks, slightly beaten
1 teaspoon vanilla
3 egg whites, stiffly beaten
8 servings

Soak bread in milk and rub through a sieve, add sugar, coconut milk, melted butter, coconut, slightly beaten egg yolks, vanilla, and stiffly beaten egg whites. Pour into a buttered mold and bake in a pan containing 1 inch of hot water for 40 to 50 minutes at 350 degrees. Turn out of mold and serve warm or cold with Caramel Sauce (Recipe 128).

209. TAPIOCA CREAM (Creme de Tapioca)

½ hour

3 cups milk
1 cup sugar
½ cup minute tapioca
¼ teaspoon salt
1 tablespoon butter
4 egg yolks
shredded coconut
6 servings

Put milk in top of a double boiler, heat, add sugar, and sprinkle in the minute tapioca. Cook until tapioca is clear, add salt and butter. Beat egg yolks, add a little of the tapioca mixture, mix and return to tapioca cream, cook until thick. Pour into individual Pyrex dishes, sprinkle coconut on top, brown quickly under broiler. Serve cold.

210. BLUMENAU GRAPE TAPIOCA (Tapioca Blumenau)

45 minutes

1 quart thick sweetened grape juice
½ cup minute tapioca
¼ teaspoon salt
sweetened whipped cream
6 servings

Put the grape juice, sweetened to your taste, in top of a double boiler; when hot, sprinkle in the tapioca and salt. Cook until tapioca is clear. Turn into a glass serving dish. Chill. When ready to serve, decorate top with the sweetened whipped cream.

211. CARIOCA PUDDING (Pudim Carioca)

1½ hours

2 cups milk
1½ cups sugar
½ cup minute tapioca
1 tablespoon butter
¾ cup coconut milk
4 egg yolks, beaten
2 egg whites, stiffly beaten
grated rind of 1 lemon
8 servings

Heat the milk and sugar in top of a double boiler, add tapioca, cook until clear, add butter, coconut milk, and egg yolks. Cool. Add the egg whites and the grated lemon rind. Pour into a buttered mold, put in a baking pan containing 1 inch of hot water, and bake for 40 minutes at 375 degrees. Serve warm or cold.

212. DOLORES CREAM (Creme Dolores)

45 minutes

1 cup butter
1½ cups sugar
1 large can peaches
12 ladyfingers
whipped cream
6 servings

Beat butter and sugar until creamy. Drain peaches, reserving juice, chop finely, and add to mixture. Soak the ladyfingers in the peach juice, arrange a layer in a buttered and wax-paper-lined mold, cover with peach cream, and continue until ingredients are used up. Chill. Turn onto glass dessert plate, cover with whipped cream.

213. COFFEE REFRIGERATOR PUDDING (Pudim de Café)

    1 hour 15 minutes
    12 egg yolks
    14 tablespoons sugar
    6 tablespoons strong coffee
    ½ pound unsalted butter
    12 ladyfingers
    whipped cream
    chopped nuts
        8 servings

Beat egg yolks with sugar until creamy, add coffee, cook in top of a double boiler until thick, stirring constantly. Cool. Add slightly softened butter and mix well. Put a layer of ladyfingers in a greased, wax-paper-lined mold, cover with coffee cream, put in another layer of ladyfingers, and finish with cream. Chill in refrigerator overnight. Unmold and decorate with whipped cream and chopped nuts.

214. BRIDE'S COUCH (Colchão de Noiva)

    1 hour 15 minutes
    4 egg whites
    9 egg yolks
    ¾ cup sugar
    ¼ teaspoon salt
    ½ teaspoon cream of tartar
    ⅔ cup flour
    powdered sugar
    jelly or Milk Pudding (Recipe 217)
        8 servings

Beat egg whites until they will stand in peaks but are not dry. Beat egg yolks until thick. Add the yolks to the whites and mix gently. Sift all dry ingredients and fold into the eggs gradually. Spread batter in a 15×10 inch jelly-roll pan which has been greased and lined with waxed paper. Bake in a moderately hot oven (350 degrees) for 15 minutes. Turn onto a clean napkin which has been generously sprinkled with powdered sugar and trim crisp edges. Spread with your favorite jelly or the Milk Pudding and roll up. Cut in slices.

215. White Manjar with Prunes and Coconut *mon-jar'* (Manjar Branco com Ameixas e Côco)

1 hour

4 cups milk
1 cup sugar
6 tablespoons cornstarch
½ teaspoon salt
1 teaspoon vanilla
2 cups shredded coconut
    8 servings

Make a cream of the milk heated in a double boiler, adding sugar mixed with cornstarch, salt, vanilla, and coconut, and cook until thick. Turn into a mold which has been rinsed with cold water. Put in refrigerator to chill. Unmold. Pour over it the following sauce:

SAUCE

1 cup cooked and pitted prunes
1 cup prune juice
1 cup water
Cook all together for 5 minutes. Cool.

216. Delicious Little Cupfuls (Copinhos Delicia)

½ hour

12 egg yolks
12 tablespoons sugar
4 teaspoons cornstarch
½ teaspoon salt
4 cups milk
½ teaspoon vanilla
2 tablespoons cocoa
2 tablespoons hot water
cinnamon
sweetened whipped cream
    8 servings

Heat milk in top of a double boiler. Beat egg yolks, sugar, cornstarch, and salt together, add to milk in a double boiler and cook until thick. Add vanilla. Put half of this mixture into custard cups. To the other half, add the cocoa, which has been dissolved in the hot water. Fill up the custard cups with the cocoa mixture and sprinkle with cinnamon. Chill. Serve with a spoonful of sweetened whipped cream on top of each.

217. MILK PUDDING (Doce de Leite)

45 minutes

2 cups sugar
¾ cup water
8 egg yolks
4 cups milk
1 teaspoon vanilla
2 tablespoons butter
10 servings

Make a syrup of sugar and water, according to Recipe 244. Cool, add egg yolks beaten in the milk. Return to flame, add vanilla and butter, and cook, stirring constantly until mixture pulls away from sides of pan. Pour in individual molds and serve chilled.

218. EGG AND ALMOND PUDDING (Doce de Ovos com Amêndoas)

1 hour

2 cups sugar
½ cup water
8 egg yolks, slightly beaten
½ cup ground almonds
6 servings

Bring sugar and water to boil and cook for 3 minutes, remove from flame and cool. Add slightly beaten egg yolks and almonds and cook over low flame, stirring constantly, until thick. Pour into individual molds and chill.

219. Young Girl's Delight (Baba de Moça)

35 minutes

3 cups sugar
1¼ cups water
1½ cups coconut milk
18 egg yolks, beaten
12 servings

Make a syrup of sugar and water, according to Recipe 244, add coconut milk, and cook 5 minutes longer. Cool. Add beaten egg yolks and cook over low flame until the mixture pulls away from the sides of the pan. Serve.

220. Quindim Coconut Pudding (Quindim Especial)

35 minutes

15 egg yolks
2 cups sugar
¾ cup coconut milk
¼ teaspoon salt
1 tablespoon melted butter
10 servings

Beat egg yolks, mix in all other ingredients, cook in top of a double boiler until thick, stirring constantly. Cool and serve.

221. Manioc Cream (Creme de Aipim)

1 hour 15 minutes

3 cups cooked manioc roots, mashed and sieved
2 cups milk
¾ cup coconut milk
¼ teaspoon salt
1 cup sugar
2 tablespoons melted butter
4 eggs, beaten
8 servings

Mix sieved manioc roots with milk, coconut milk, salt, sugar, melted butter and beaten eggs, and sieve again. Turn mixture into a greased baking dish, and bake in a pan containing 1 inch of hot water for about 40 minutes in a 375-degree oven, or until mixture is set. Serve warm or cold.

222. PRUNE CREAM (Creme de Ameixas)

1 hour

1 cup cooked prunes
2 cups prune juice
2 cups sugar
2 cups milk
2 tablespoons cornstarch
½ cup sugar
½ teaspoon salt
3 eggs
1 teaspoon vanilla
6 servings

Pit the prunes, cook the prune juice and sugar together for 10 minutes, add the pitted prunes. Cook for 5 minutes more. Cool. Heat the milk in the top of the double boiler, sift in the cornstarch, sugar, and salt, which have been well mixed, cook until thick. Beat eggs slightly, put a few tablespoons of the custard mixture in the eggs and mix well, return this to custard in double boiler and cook until thickened. Add vanilla. Pour into a mold which has been rinsed with cold water. Chill. Unmold on a glass dessert plate, pour the prunes over it. Serve very cold.

223. Baked Prune Cream (Creme de Ameixas ao Fôrno)

1 hour 15 minutes
6 servings

Follow Recipe 222 exactly, leaving out the egg whites in the custard mixture. Beat the whites with 3 tablespoons of sugar. Put layers of the custard and prunes in a greased baking dish, cover with the meringue, and put into a 375-degree oven for 15 minutes, or until meringue is brown.

224. Banana Pudding (Sobremesa de Bananas)

1 hour

2 cups flour
2 tablespoons sugar
1 teaspoon salt
2 teaspoons baking powder
3 tablespoons butter
1 egg
⅔ cup milk
bananas, cubed
sugar
cinnamon
8 servings

Sift flour, sugar, salt, and baking powder together, work in butter and the egg beaten with the milk. Spread about ½ inch thick on a buttered baking pan, cover top with cubed bananas, and sprinkle with sugar and cinnamon. Bake for about ½ hour in a 375-degree oven. Serve with Hot Sauce, as follows:

HOT SAUCE

¼ cup sugar
2 tablespoons flour
2 cups boiling water
3 tablespoons butter
½ teaspoon salt
1 teaspoon vanilla
brandy or port wine

Mix sugar and flour and sift into the boiling water, stirring constantly. Add butter, salt, and vanilla and cook for a few minutes. Add a little brandy or port wine if you wish.

225. BANANA AND EGG CUSTARD (Pudim de Banana com Ovos)

1 hour 20 minutes

6 eggs
2 cups sugar
1 cup mashed bananas
2 tablespoons melted butter
4 tablespoons flour
1 teaspoon cinnamon
6 servings

Beat egg yolks with sugar, mix in mashed bananas, melted butter, flour, and cinnamon. Beat egg whites until stiff and fold into first mixture. Turn into a buttered mold and bake in a pan containing 1 inch of hot water for about 40 minutes, at 375 degrees.

226. EASY-COOKED BANANAS IN CARAMEL SAUCE (Bananas Cozidas)

15 minutes

½ cup sugar
1 cup hot water
4 to 6 bananas
4 to 6 servings

Caramelize the sugar in a heavy frying pan, add the hot water, and boil for 1 minute. Lay peeled bananas in pan, cover, and cook until bananas are soft and puffed up. Serve immediately while still hot—the bananas wilt if they stand.

227. EASIER-COOKED BANANAS (Bananas Cozidas)

10 minutes

bananas
hot water
sugar
cinnamon

Put desired number of bananas in a kettle without peeling, and cover with hot water. Cook until bananas are tender, or until a fork pierces them easily. Serve immediately, 1 or 2 bananas to a person, slitting open the skin and sprinkling with sugar and cinnamon.

228. ELZA'S PORT-WINE GELATIN (Gelatina Elza com Vinho do Porto)

45 minutes
1 package unflavored gelatin
1 cup milk
⅓ cup sugar
2 tablespoons port wine
4 egg whites, stiffly beaten
6 servings

Sprinkle gelatin on top of cold milk and cook over low flame until it curdles. Cool and add sugar, wine and beaten egg whites. Pour into mold which has been rinsed with cold water, and put in refrigerator to set. Serve with the following sauce:

SAUCE

4 egg yolks
2 cups milk
6 tablespoons sugar
1 teaspoon vanilla

Beat egg yolks, add milk, sugar, and vanilla, cook until thick in top of a double boiler, stirring constantly. Chill.

229. LADYFINGER GELATIN (Gelatina de Biscoitos)

1 hour
8 ladyfingers
4 cups milk
4 egg yolks
6 tablespoons sugar
2 packages gelatin
½ cup cold water
6 egg whites, beaten
sweetened whipped cream
8 servings

Crumble ladyfingers into the cold milk and soak for a few minutes. Beat egg yolks with sugar and add to ladyfingers and milk. Cook in double boiler until it thickens, stirring well. Have gelatin soaking in cold water and add, stirring together until gelatin is melted. Remove from flame and fold in the beaten egg whites. Pour into a mold and put into the refrigerator to set. Unmold and serve with sweetened whipped cream.

230. DELICIOUS APPLE GELATIN (Gelatina de Maçã)

    2 hours
    1 glass strawberry jelly or jam
    15 ladyfingers
    1½ envelopes unflavored gelatin
    ½ cup water
    1 cup milk
    6 egg whites
    9 tablespoons of sugar
    6 egg yolks
    3 apples
    2 tablespoons crème de menthe
    2 tablespoons cognac
    sweetened whipped cream
    maraschino cherries (optional)
    8 servings

Line a mold with strawberry jam or jelly and arrange ladyfingers on bottom and sides of the mold over the jelly. Set aside. Sprinkle the gelatin on the cold water, add to milk and heat until scalded and gelatin is dissolved. Put in refrigerator until it begins to harden. Beat egg whites stiff and add sugar. Beat egg yolks and add to the whites. Peel and slice the apples very thin and add to the egg mixture. Mix in the crème de menthe and cognac, and the gelatin, which is beginning to harden. Pour this into the jelly-and-ladyfinger-lined mold, and put in refrigerator to harden. Unmold on plate and decorate with sweetened whipped cream, blobs of strawberry jam or jelly, or maraschino cherries.

231. CLARITA'S PINEAPPLE GELATIN WITH PRUNE CUSTARD (Creme Clarita)

1½ hours

2 envelopes unflavored gelatin
3 cups cooked sweetened pineapple juice
1 cup cooked pineapple pulp
1 cup cooked prunes
1¼ cups sugar
½ cup water
6 egg yolks, beaten
6 egg whites
    8 servings

Sprinkle the gelatin on the pineapple juice, heat until gelatin is dissolved, add the pineapple pulp. Pour into mold and put into refrigerator to set. Remove pits from prunes. Make a syrup of ¾ cup sugar and the water, according to Recipe 244, cool, and add beaten egg yolks. Cook over low flame until thick. Beat the egg whites, add ½ cup sugar, beat until stiff, fold in the egg-yolk mixture and prunes. Cool. Unmold gelatin, pour over it the prune-and-egg custard.

232. FRUIT-WINE GELATIN FOR THIRTY-FIVE SERVINGS (Gelatina de Frutas)

1½ hours

12 envelopes gelatin
8 cups water
4 cups white wine
1 can pineapple juice
1 teaspoon caraway seeds
1 teaspoon cinnamon
1 teaspoon cloves
4 cups sugar
8 cups orange juice
4 tablespoons lemon juice
2 egg whites, lightly beaten
sweetened whipped cream
maraschino cherries
    35 servings

Sprinkle the gelatin on the 8 cups of water, which have been put into a wide pan. When the gelatin is saturated with water, put over a low flame and heat until gelatin is melted. Add wine, pineapple juice, caraway seeds, cinnamon, cloves, and sugar, and bring to boil for 3 minutes; add orange and lemon juice and heat again. Remove from flame and while still hot, stir in the beaten egg whites. Let stand for ½ hour, then strain through a wet cloth. Pour in large molds which have been rinsed with cold water, or into individual molds. Chill until it hardens. Unmold. Serve decorated with sweetened whipped cream and maraschino cherries.

233. PINK CREAM (Creme Rosado)

45 minutes
1 package strawberry gelatin
2 cups boiling water
6 eggs
6 tablespoons sugar
whipped cream
6 servings

Dissolve gelatin in boiling water in top of a double boiler, beat egg yolks, put a little of the dissolved gelatin in the egg yolks, mix, and return to double boiler. Cook until thick. Remove from fire and pour over the egg whites which have been beaten stiff with sugar. Turn into mold which has been rinsed with cold water, put into refrigerator to set. Unmold. Serve with whipped cream.

234. DIPLOMAT PUDDING (Pudim Diplomata)

1 hour 15 minutes
1 envelope unflavored gelatin
4 cups milk
10 eggs
1 tablespoon butter
2 cups sugar
1 teaspoon vanilla
2 cups cooked sugared prunes with juice
sweetened whipped cream
8 servings

Sprinkle gelatin on cold milk, put in top of a double boiler, and heat, stirring, until gelatin is melted. Beat eggs slightly, add a few spoons of the gelatin to milk mixture, mix well, and return to double boiler. Add butter, sugar, and vanilla and cook until thick. Pour into mold. Put in refrigerator to set. Pit and sieve the prunes. Turn gelatin mold onto deep plate, and cover with sieved prunes. Decorate with sweetened whipped cream.

235. AVOCADO CREAM   (Creme de Abacate)

    10 minutes

    3 ripe avocados
    6 tablespoons sugar
    juice of 1 lemon
    6 servings

Peel the avocados, remove seeds, and put in blender with sugar and lemon juice, or mash and press through a sieve. Put into a glass bowl, or in sherbet cups and chill thoroughly in the refrigerator. Serve.

236. AVOCADO CREAM WITH ICE CREAM (Creme de Abacate com Sorvete)

    10 minutes

    3 ripe avocados
    3 tablespoons sugar
    juice of 1 lemon
    1 cup vanilla ice cream
    8 servings

Peel the avocados, remove seeds, and put in blender with sugar, lemon juice, and ice cream. Serve thoroughly chilled.

237. BANANA CREAM (Creme de Banana)

    10 minutes

    6 mashed bananas
    1 cup heavy sweet cream
    juice of 1 lemon
    1 teaspoon vanilla
    8 servings

186

Put all ingredients in blender until smooth. Serve in sherbet cups.

238. FRUIT SALAD (Salada de Frutas)

Cut up all fruits available—fresh or canned pineapple chunks, orange sections, fresh or canned peaches, seeded grapes, cubes of apples, dipped in lemon juice, chunks of peeled and seeded papaya, large cherries, cubes of banana. Be careful to keep pieces whole and not crushed. Pile carefully into large individual serving dishes. Pour a few tablespoons of the mixed fruit juices over each dish, and garnish with a sprig of mint. You may mix a little rum in the juices to be poured over the fruit, or a tablespoon of crème de menthe.

239. TROPICAL ICE (Gelo Tropical)

Make a fruit salad as above, and put into the freezing tray of the refrigerator. Pour over it plenty of the well-sweetened juice. Serve when it begins to freeze around the edges of tray.

240. FRUIT SHERBET (Sorvete de Frutas)

40 minutes
⅓ cup lemon juice
2 cups mashed bananas
⅓ cup orange juice
½ cup light corn syrup
⅛ teaspoon salt
1 egg white
⅓ cup sugar
⅓ cup milk
¼ cup maraschino-cherry juice
½ cup coarsely chopped maraschino cherries
½ cup crushed pineapple
½ teaspoon grated orange rind
8 servings

Mix lemon juice with bananas, then add orange juice, corn syrup, and salt. Beat egg white stiff but not dry, gradually beat in sugar. Fold into banana mixture. Add milk, cherry juice, cherries, pineapple, and orange rind. Pour into refrigerator tray and freeze until mixture is almost firm. Place in chilled bowl and beat. Return to tray and continue freezing until firm.

241. AVOCADO ICE CREAM (Sorvete de Abacate)

½ hour

2 ripe avocados, peeled and pitted
juice of 1 lemon
1 cup sugar
1 cup whipped cream
6 servings

Mash and sieve avocados or put in blender, add lemon, sugar and the whipped cream. Put in freezing tray and freeze until firm.

242. LEMON ICE (Sorvete de Limão)

40 minutes

2½ cups water
¾ cups corn syrup
1 cup sugar
¼ teaspoon salt
1 tablespoon grated lemon rind
⅔ cup lemon juice
yellow or green coloring
6 to 8 servings

Combine water, corn syrup, sugar, salt, and lemon rind in a saucepan. Stir until sugar is dissolved, bring to a boil, and boil for 5 minutes without stirring. Cool. Add lemon juice. Strain to remove lemon rind. Tint a delicate yellow or green shade. Freeze in a refrigerator tray until firm throughout. Remove to chilled bowl, break up with a wooden spoon, and beat with rotary beater or mixer until light. Return to refrigerator to complete freezing.

243. TROPICAL FRUIT TRAY (Prato de Frutas)

1 whole fresh pineapple
strawberries
oranges
avocados
1 whole fresh papaya
black cherries
any other available fruit
fern leaves

Wash all the fruit, scrubbing the pineapple with a brush, and washing the prickly leaves. Peel the pineapple, but leave on leaves. Leave stems on strawberries. Peel oranges, using a sharp knife and cutting off white skin, so that pulp is exposed. Line platter or tray with fern leaves or any other leaves that you may have, put pineapple in center, supported by peeled oranges, avocados, or other fruit. Cut papaya in wedges and leave seeds, as they are very decorative. Arrange slices of papaya on plate. Tuck cherries and strawberries in among the fruit. Serve fruit on large plates, lifting off a a share of each for each person. Pineapple can be sliced, avocados cut in half and served with sugar and a squeeze of lemon and scooped out with a spoon. This fruit tray makes a beautiful decoration for a buffet supper.

CANDY

Here are the recipes of the candies that play such an important part in every *festa*. They are rather simple sweets, not too rich, and pretty to look at with their delicate colors and amusing shapes —not to mention their amusing names. Get a supply of paper cups, in all colors and of gold and silver, and lace doilies of gold and silver. Arrange the sweets on the plates, with care to make each plate a work of art. If you are skilled at making paper flowers, nestle the dainties among masses of the flowers or put them on sparkling glass or silver plates. The Almond Easter Rabbits will be appropriate for a children's party, and the Almond and Apricot Delights will add color (Recipes 250 and 252). Try making some of our Pé de Moleque (Urchin's Foot) (Recipe 266), which is the Brazilian counterpart of peanut brittle. This is one of the commonest of all Brazilian candies and is sold in every sweetshop as well as on the streets, especially in north Brazil. Cocadas (Recipe 261) made of sugar and coconut are perhaps just as common, since coconut is plentiful and cheap. These last two sweets are the ones you will see the street urchins munching as they sell their papers, or their little "pokes" of freshly roasted peanuts, which they keep hot over improvised charcoal stoves made from kerosene tins. Even in the cities on crowded corners, or where there is a line of people buying tickets for the cinema, the little businessman plies his trade, keeping the peanuts warm on his stove, and incidentally, himself, if it happens to be a chilly day in the winter.

MAKING BRAZILIAN CANDIES

The almonds and Brazil nuts used in the recipes are blanched, and when the recipe calls for them to be ground, this should be very, very fine. There are many recipes which call for a syrup, mixed with eggs and other ingredients. Except when the recipe calls for other treatment, the syrup is cooked and cooled and the eggs are mixed in without beating. Always use a heavy pan and cook over a very low flame. If the mixture sticks to your hands when forming into balls, moisten your hands with unbeaten egg white. Use buttered tongs to hold candies when dipping into glaze, but if you have no tongs, drop in the balls and remove with a buttered sharp-tined fork.

244. BASIC SYRUP   (Calda Grossa)

2½ cups sugar
1 cup water

Boil the sugar and water until it spins a thread, stirring occasionally.

Since a number of recipes require syrup, you may consult this recipe when you need it. The quantities of sugar and water may vary, or it may be necessary to boil the mixture a little longer to obtain the proper syrup.

245. ALMOND BALLS (Massa de Amêndoas)

1 hour
2 cups confectioners' sugar
2 cups ground blanched almonds
1 egg white
24 candied cherries
  About 24 balls

Add 1 tablespoon sugar to the ground almonds. Grind again, or until very fine. Add the egg white and the rest of the sugar. You should have a smooth paste. Make small balls of the paste and top each with a cherry.

246. ALMOND AND NUT ROLLS (Massa de Amêndoas e Castanhas do Pará)

2 hours

3 cups sugar
1¼ cups water
1 cup ground blanched almonds
25 egg yolks
1 tablespoon butter
prune jam or jelly
About 30 servings

Make a syrup of sugar and water, according to Recipe 244. Combine almonds, egg yolks and butter, add to syrup, and return to flame. Cook until the mixture pulls away from the sides of the pan, stirring constantly. Cool. Spread evenly on a sugared board, cover with a layer of prune jam or jelly. Roll up and wrap in aluminum foil. Leave it until it is firm, then slice.

247. ALMOND CREAMS (Amanteigados)

1½ hours

2½ cups sugar
1 cup water
3 cups ground blanched almonds
12 egg yolks
6 egg whites, unbeaten
6 egg whites, stiffly beaten
crystallized sugar
About 36 squares

Make a syrup of the sugar and water, according to Recipe 244, and cool. Mix in the almonds, egg yolks, unbeaten egg whites, and fold in the 6 beaten egg whites. Place in a square buttered baking dish and bake for 20 minutes at 300 degrees. Cool and cut into small squares. Roll each in crystallized sugar and place in small decorative paper cups.

248. CARAMEL-GLAZED ALMOND CREAMS (Amanteigados com Caramelo)

1½ hours

2 cups sugar
¾ cup water
2 cups grated blanched almonds
7 egg yolks
2 egg whites
crystallized sugar
About 30 balls

Make a syrup of sugar and water (Recipe 244). Add grated almonds, stir, and remove from flame. Cool. Add unbeaten egg yolks and egg whites and return to flame and cook, stirring constantly until the mixture begins to pull away from the sides of the pan. Cool. Shape into small balls, sprinkle with sugar, and place on (greased) baking sheet. Let stand until next day, then bake for 5 minutes at 400 degrees, or until golden brown. Dip in caramel syrup and put on buttered marble or cooky sheet to cool. Serve in small paper cups.

CARAMEL SYRUP

2 cups sugar
½ cup water
2 tablespoons white wine

Cook sugar and water, stirring very little, until it spins a thread. Add wine and cook a minute longer, without stirring. It should be a golden color. Keep hot over hot water. Dip each ball in syrup.

249. ALMOND "HAMS" (Presuntinhos)

1½ hours

1 cup sugar
⅓ cup water
1 cup ground almonds
3 tablespoons cocoa
3 tablespoons confectioners' sugar
18 "hams"

Make a syrup of the sugar and water (Recipe 244). Add almonds and cook until the mixture pulls away from the sides of the pan, stirring constantly. Cool. Divide in two parts. Work the cocoa into one part, and the confectioners' sugar into the other. Make the little "hams" of both parts, using the dark and light to represent the skin and fat part of the ham. Put each one in a little silver cup.

250. ALMOND EASTER RABBITS (Coelhinhos de Amêndoas)

1½ hours

3 cups sugar
1¼ cups water
1 cup ground blanched almonds
4 whole eggs
2 egg yolks
confectioners' sugar
1 dozen whole almonds, cut in slivers
1 tablespoon cocoa
6 candied cherries, cut in tiny pieces
About 24 rabbits

Make a syrup of sugar and water (Recipe 244). Cool. Add ground almonds, whole eggs, and egg yolks. Cook until the mixture pulls away from the sides of the pan and cool. Roll into small balls, mold them into rabbit shapes, and dip in confectioners' sugar. Add 2 slivers of almond for the ears, and paint the eyes with the cocoa mixed with a tiny bit of water. Make the tongue with a piece of cherry. You may make these larger or smaller, as you wish.

251. ALMOND SUGAR WONDERS (Maravilhas de Açucar)

1½ hours

1 cup sugar
2 tablespoons ground blanched almonds
5 egg yolks
1 tablespoon flour
red jelly
  About 18 patties

Mix sugar, almonds, egg yolks, and flour. Cook in heavy pan until the mass pulls away from the sides of the pan, stirring constantly. Cool and shape into patties and decorate each with a dab of colorful jelly.

252. APRICOT AND ALMOND DELIGHTS (Delícia de Damasco e Amêndoas)

1½ hours

2 cups sugar
¾ cup water
15 cooked, drained apricots
2 tablespoons butter
2½ cups ground blanched almonds
12 egg yolks
6 egg whites
crystallized sugar
dried apricots
  About 36 balls

Make a syrup of sugar and water (Recipe 244). Cool. Press apricots through a fine sieve. Add all ingredients except crystallized sugar to the syrup and mix well. Cook over low flame stirring constantly, until mass pulls away from sides of pan. Form into ball, and leave until next day. Then make small balls and dip each in crystallized sugar and decorate with a tiny bit of dried apricot.

253. APRICOT PATTIES (Docinhos de Damasco)

1½ hours

1 pound dried apricots
1½ cups sugar
About 24 patties

Cook and mash apricots. Mix with sugar and cook until mixture pulls away from the sides of the pan. Cool. Make small patties and roll in crystallized sugar.

254. BRAZIL-NUT CANDIES (Docinhos de Castanha do Pará)

1½ hours

2½ cups sugar
1 cup water
1 tablespoon butter
3 tablespoons ground Brazil nuts
2 teaspoons cocoa
18 toasted Brazil nuts
About 18 rolls

Make a syrup of sugar and water (Recipe 244). Add butter and ground nuts. Cook slowly, stirring constantly, until the mixture pulls away from the sides of the pan, and add cocoa, dissolved in a little water. Cool and shape into little rolls and stick a Brazil nut on top of each.

255. BETHLEHEM SQUARES (Docinhos de Belém)

1 hour

1½ cups ground Brazil nuts
1½ cups sugar
8 eggs
1 tablespoon butter
crystallized sugar
18 squares

Combine all ingredients and mix very well. Spread on a greased baking sheet and bake for 20 to 25 minutes at 300 degrees. Cool, cut into small squares, and dip in crystallized sugar.

256. GLAZED BRAZIL-NUT BALLS (Bolas de Castanha do Pará)

2 hours

2 cups sugar
¾ cup water
1 cup ground Brazil nuts
8 egg yolks
1 teaspoon vanilla
1 recipe Caramel Syrup (Recipe 248)
About 24 balls

Make a syrup of sugar and water (Recipe 244), cool, and add rest of ingredients. Cook until the mixture pulls away from the sides of the pan. Cool and make little balls. Dip in Caramel Syrup and put on buttered marble or cooky sheet to cool. Serve in little paper cups.

257. BRAZIL-NUT BONBONS (Bombons de Castanha do Pará)

1½ hours

2 cups ground toasted Brazil nuts
3 cups sugar
¼ teaspoon salt
2 tablespoons cocoa
6 eggs
4 tablespoons butter
12 walnuts, cut in pieces
About 24 balls

Put the nuts, sugar, salt, cocoa, eggs and 2 tablespoons butter in a heavy saucepan and cook, stirring constantly until the mixture pulls away from the sides of the pan. Remove from flame and stir in the remaining butter. This mixture should be very smooth. Cool. Make small balls, press a piece of walnut on top of each ball, and put into small paper cups. Should the mixture become too hard as you work, work in a little more butter.

258. "I WANT MORE" ("Quero Mais")

    1½ hours

    2 cups milk
    ¼ teaspoon salt
    4 tablespoons cocoa
    18 tablespoons sugar
    6 eggs, well beaten
    2 cups ground English walnuts
    crystallized sugar
      About 24 rolls

Put milk, salt and cocoa, and 9 tablespoons of the sugar over flame and bring to boiling point. Let cool and add eggs, the remaining sugar, and nuts. Cook over low flame until the mixture pulls away from the sides of the pan. Spread on buttered marble or cooky sheet to cool. Make small rolls and dip each in crystallized sugar. Serve in small paper cups.

259. COCONUT APPLES (Maçãzinhas de Côco)

    2 hours

    1½ cups shredded coconut
    1 cup sugar
    4 tablespoons butter
    5 eggs
    5 egg yolks
    1 recipe Caramel Syrup (Recipe 248)
      About 24 "apples"

Mix all ingredients and cook, stirring constantly, until mixture pulls away from the sides of the pan. Remove from heat and cool. Shape into small "apples" and let stand for 1 day. Then dip into Caramel Syrup and put on buttered marble or cooky sheet to cool. Put each in small paper cup.

260. COCONUT PEARS (Perinhas de Côco)

1½ hours

4 egg yolks
2 cups sugar
2 cups freshly grated coconut
1 egg white
24 almonds
  About 24 "pears"

Mix egg yolks, sugar, coconut, and egg white, and cook over low heat, stirring constantly, until mixture pulls away from the sides of the pan. Let the mixture stand for 1 day. Moisten your hands in egg white and make small pear-shaped candies, put them on a greased cooky sheet, and bake for 20 to 25 minutes at 300 degrees. Stick an almond on top of each for "stem."

261. COCADAS (ko-kah'-dahs)

1 hour

1½ pounds crystallized sugar
1 cup water
1 pound grated coconut or 2 fresh coconuts, grated
  About 24 cocadas

Make a syrup of sugar and water (Recipe 244). Pour it over the grated coconut and let this mixture stand for 1 day. Then make patties of this and roll in sugar. Put them in the sun to dry or dry for a few minutes in a very low oven.

262. TWO LOVES (Dois Amores)

1 hour 15 minutes

2 cups sugar
¾ cup water
2 cups shredded coconut
cake coloring
crystallized sugar
  About 12 "sandwiches"

Make a syrup of sugar and water (Recipe 244). Pour over coconut and mix. Divide in two parts, color each with a different color, very delicately. Make flat patties and press 2 patties together, making little sandwiches. Turn in crystallized sugar.

263. SHE AND I (Ela e Eu)

1½ hours

1 can sweetened condensed milk (14 ounces)
3 tablespoons cocoa
2 tablespoons butter
¼ teaspoon salt
2 packages granulated chocolate (1½ cups)
About 24

Cook condensed milk and cocoa, until the mixture pulls away from the sides of the pan. Add butter and salt, mix in well, and remove from flame. When cool, make little balls and roll in granulated chocolate. Place in small paper cups.

264. LITTLE KISSES (Beijinhos)

1½ hours

1½ cups sugar
½ cup water
2 tablespoons butter
12 eggs
2 tablespoons flour
candied cherries
crystallized sugar
About 18 balls

Make a syrup of sugar and water (Recipe 244). Remove from flame and add butter and cool. Mix eggs and flour, add to syrup, and cook until the mixture pulls away from the sides of the pan. Set aside until next day. Make small balls, roll in sugar, and decorate with cherry. This recipe may be used as a filling for "Newlyweds" (Recipe 184).

265. MISCELLANEOUS (Miscelanea)

   1½ hours

   2 cups dried pitted prunes
   2 cups pitted dates
   6 dried apricots
   4 slices canned pineapple
   ½ cup sugar
   ½ cup port wine
   crystallized sugar
   1 recipe Caramel Syrup, Recipe 248 (optional)
      About 36 balls

Grind all fruit and mix with sugar and wine. Make small balls,
roll them in crystallized sugar or dip in Caramel Syrup, and put
on buttered marble or cooky sheet to dry.

266. PÉ DE MOLEQUE (*peh-day-mole-eck'-ay*)

   1 hour

   3 cups water
   2 pounds brown sugar
   1 pound whole roasted peanuts
   1 teaspoon salt
      About 24 patties

Boil water and sugar until it spins a thread. Put in peanuts and
salt and mix lightly. Let cool on a greased marble or cooky sheet.
Make patties, using a tablespoon as a measure.

267. PINEAPPLE BALLS (Balas de Abacaxi)

   2 hours

   3 cups sugar
   1¼ cups water
   3 slices pineapple, grated
   3 egg yolks
   2 teaspoons cornstarch
   crystallized sugar
      About 24 balls

Make a syrup of sugar and water (Recipe 244) and cool. Then
add pineapple, egg yolks, and cornstarch, and cook until the mixture

pulls away from the sides of the pan. Cool. Make small balls, roll in crystallized sugar, and put in small paper cups.

268. PUMPKIN SWEETS (Docinhos de Abóbora)

> 1 hour 15 minutes
> 1 can pumpkin or yellow squash
> equal weight of sugar
> 3 tablespoons whole cloves
> 1 stick cinnamon
> crystallized sugar
>> About 18 patties

Mix pumpkin and sugar and cook with cloves and cinnamon until mixture is thick and stands up. Be careful that it does not stick to the bottom of the pan. Let it stand for 1 day, then make into patties, using tablespoon as measure. Let them dry in sun or in a very low oven. Roll in crystallized sugar.

269. BALANGANDÃS (bahl-an'-gan-dans)

> 1½ hours
> 2 cups sugar
> 2 cups ground walnuts
> 1 cup milk
> 5 egg yolks
> candied cherries
> raw prunes (optional)
> wine (optional)
>> 24 balangandans

Mix all ingredients and cook, stirring constantly, until the mixture pulls away from the sides of the pan. Roll out ½ inch thick on a sugared board. Cut with 1-inch cooky cutter. Place a cherry on top of each. You may vary this recipe by wrapping each around a piece of raw prune which has been soaked in wine.

270. MOTHER-IN-LAW'S EYES (Olhos de Sogra)

2 hours

36 whole raw prunes
½ pound blanched almonds
about 1 cup sugar
1 egg white
36 candies

Slit one side of each prune and remove pit carefully, so as to keep prune whole. Grind the blanched almonds 3 times in the blender, adding a tablespoon of sugar after the first grinding. Then work in the white of egg and keep on working in sugar until it becomes a smooth mass. With a teaspoon fill each prune, or make the filling as follows:

FILLING

½ pound sugar
¾ cup water
4 egg whites
12 egg yolks

Make a syrup of the sugar and water (Recipe 244) and cool. Mix the egg whites and yolks and strain into the syrup; then mix well, put over flame, and cook, stirring constantly, until the bottom of the pan shows. Cool, and stuff prunes.

GLAZE

2 cups sugar
½ cup water
2 tablespoons vinegar

After filling the prunes with either mixture, make a glaze with the sugar and water, cooking for 5 minutes and then adding vinegar. Cook until it spins a long hair. Dip each prune in this glaze and let cool on greased marble or greased cooky sheet. Serve in pretty gold paper cups.

271. BRIGADIERS (Brigadeiros)

1½ hours

2 cans of sweetened condensed milk
½ pound bitter chocolate, finely shaved
½ teaspoon salt
granulated chocolate
30 balls

Put the condensed milk, bitter chocolate, and salt in a heavy pan and cook, stirring constantly until you can see the bottom of the pan. Cool. Make little balls and roll in granulated chocolate. Or you may let them stand for a day and then dip in a glaze (Recipe 248).

272. GOLDEN "FIGS" (Figos de Ouro)

1 hour

2 cups grated American cheese
4 egg yolks
2 cups sugar
¾ cup water
crystallized sugar
About 18 "figs"

Mix cheese and egg yolks and mold into little "figs." Make a syrup of sugar and water (Recipe 244) and boil the figs in the syrup until firm. Remove from syrup, cool, and roll in crystallized sugar.

273. COCONUT AND PINEAPPLE BALLS (Bolinhos de Côco e Abacaxi)

2 hours

2 ripe pineapples
1 coconut, grated
3 cups sugar
crystallized sugar
36 balls

Grind the pineapple in the grinder, catching the juice in a bowl. Put the pineapple pulp, the juice, grated coconut, and sugar in a heavy pan, mix well, and cook until you can see the bottom of the pan, stirring frequently. Cool and make into little balls. Roll each in crystallized sugar and put into little paper cups.

274. Coconut and Sweet-potato Croquettes (Croquetinhas de Côco e Batata Doce)

2 hours

2 cups mashed sweet potatoes
1 grated coconut
1½ cups sugar
3 tablespoons cocoa
crystallized sugar
36 croquettes

Mix all the ingredients and put on the fire to cook, stirring constantly until you can see the bottom of the pan. Form into little croquettes, roll in crystallized sugar, and put into little paper cups.

275. Chocolate Nut Squares (Docinhos de Chocolate e Nozes)

1 hour

3 cups sugar
1 cup rich milk
½ cup cocoa
2 tablespoons butter
2 cups ground nuts
½ teaspoon salt
24 squares

Put the sugar, milk, cocoa, and butter in a heavy pan and bring to a boil. Cook for 5 minutes, add the nuts, and continue cooking, stirring constantly, until you can see the bottom of the pan. Add the salt, remove from fire, and keep on stirring until thick. Turn out on greased marble or cooky sheet. Cut in squares.

276. Sweet-potato Gumdrops (Gelatina de Batata Doce)

1½ hours

4 cups mashed sweet potatoes
4 cups sugar
1 cinnamon stick
6 whole cloves
1 envelope unflavored gelatin
½ cup cold water
crystallized sugar
     24 balls

Cook mashed sweet potatoes and sugar together, stirring constantly until the mixture stands away from the sides of the pan. Add cinnamon, cloves, and gelatin, which has been soaked in the cold water. Stir until gelatin is well dissolved. Let stand for 24 hours, then make into any shape—balls, or rolls—and roll in crystallized sugar.

COFFEE

No one knows exactly when and how it was discovered that coffee has such delicious and energy-giving qualities, but there are many interesting legends. I like the one about the Sheik Omar, who because of differences of opinion with his superiors, was exiled to the desert in Arabia. Without food, he ate grasses and herbs to keep himself alive. When he tried the pretty red berries of the bushes that grew all around him, he felt that he had been reborn, with a sense of well-being that he had never felt before, just as you and I feel after our first cup of coffee in the morning. He was sure that the fruit had some magical property. When he toasted and boiled the berries in water, he found the results even better. Visited by the sick, he administered to them the miraculous potion, which alleviated and cured their ills. Soon the fame of this drink spread all over, and his poor retreat became a center of pilgrimages from all over, until he was finally invited to return to Mecca, where he entered triumphantly amid the delirious applause of the multitudes. A monastery was built in his honor and later he was sanctified.

277. Good Brazilian Coffee

Use the fine powdered coffee, buy it in small quantities, and keep it tightly covered after the container is opened. You will need a cloth bag, made according to the dimensions given in the sketch. Use 2 cups of boiling water with 3 heaping tablespoons of powdered coffee. Put the coffee in a saucepan, pour the boiling water over it, let it stand on a low flame for 2 or 3 minutes, not boiling, stirring constantly. Pour this into the cloth bag, which is set in the coffeepot, so that the liquid drains into the pot. Keep the coffeepot in a pan of boiling water to keep it hot. We use small coffeepots, since we drink our coffee in small demitasse cups, or diluted with hot milk, so that it is not necessary to make a large amount at a time.

278. Coffee with Milk (Café com Leite)

10 minutes

Coffee with milk is usually made about "half and half." Half fill your coffee cup with the hot coffee, fill up the cup with hot milk. You may like it light or dark and may vary proportions accordingly. Sweeten it according to taste, or serve without sugar. You may make your American-type coffee double-strength for this recipe.

279. Iced Coffee (Café Gelado)

10 minutes
cracked ice
coffee
whipped cream
sugar

Put cracked ice in glass, fill with coffee infusion, add a large spoonful of whipped cream and sugar to suit your taste.

280. Spanish Coffee Cooler (Refresco de Café à Espanhola)

½ hour

1 cup sugar
1 cup boiling water
1 quart of coffee infusion
1 cup light cream
vanilla ice cream
    6 to 8 servings

Caramelize the sugar in a heavy pan, pour the boiling water over it, stir until the lumps are all dissolved, and cook 2 minutes. Cool, add the coffee and cream, pour into tall glasses over balls of ice cream.

281. Coffee Cocktail (Coquetel de Café)

15 minutes

1 egg yolk
1 tablespoon sugar
1 cup strong coffee
1 cup port wine
½ cup brandy
1 cup cream
½ cup crushed ice
    6 servings

Beat egg yolk well, beat in other ingredients, and shake with crushed ice.

282. Brazilian Hot or Cold Chocolate (Chocolate à Brasileira)

20 minutes

2 squares semisweet chocolate
1 cup strong coffee
3 tablespoons sugar
1 pinch of salt
3 cups milk
whipped cream
    6 servings

Cut up chocolate and put in a double boiler with the coffee to melt, mixing well. Add sugar and salt, add the milk a little at a time, until all is smooth. Beat with automatic beater until foamy. Serve hot or cold, with whipped cream if desired.

283. COFFEE CAKE (Bôlo de Café)

1 hour 15 minutes

1 cup butter
2 cups brown sugar
4 eggs, well beaten
1 teaspoon salt
1 cup strong coffee
2 cups flour
1 cup rice flour
1½ teaspoons baking powder
20 servings

Beat butter and sugar together until creamy, add eggs and salt. Add the coffee and flours sifted with baking powder alternately, beat well and pour into greased and floured loaf cake pan. Bake 40 minutes at 350 degrees.

COCKTAILS and PUNCH

They say that in Rio de Janeiro "There are six months of hot weather and six months of summer." Even in the cooler zones, summers are long, and with lots of fruit, the result is "cool drinks." Brazilians generally prefer soft drinks, beer (some of the best in the world), coffee, and fruit drinks to stronger potions. Some of the tropical fruits here which make luscious punches and sherbets are not obtainable in the United States, but the following recipes include ingredients available to you. Don't overlook the Coconut Cocktail (Recipe 297), which is prepared in the coconut shell.

284. MATE TEA *mah'-tay* (Chá de Mate)

½ hour

3 tablespoons *mate* tea
3 tablespoons sugar
4½ cups boiling water
1 tablespoon lemon juice
ice cubes
    6 servings

Place *mate* mixed with sugar in a jar which has a good cover. Pour over it the boiling water, leave to soak for 20 minutes. Strain, add lemon juice, and put in refrigerator to cool. Serve in glasses with a cube of ice in each.

285. Coconut Cooler (Refresco de Côco)

10 minutes

¾ cup coconut milk
1 cup water
½ cup kümmel
sugar
crushed ice
4 servings

Mix all ingredients and sugar to suit your taste, beat well, and pour into glasses. Serve with straws.

286. Copacabana Punch (Ponche Copacabana)

40 minutes

2 apples
1 pineapple
2 peaches
juice of 2 oranges
½ cup Cointreau
½ cup curaçao
1 tablespoon sugar
2 bottles soda water
2 bottles champagne
25 servings

Cut up all the fruit, add orange juice, pour over it the Cointreau and curaçao, sugar and soda water. Put it into the refrigerator for ½ hour. When ready to serve, add 2 bottles of champagne. Serve in small crystal glasses.

287. PINEAPPLE PUNCH (Ponche de Abacaxi)

35 minutes
1 pineapple
4 glasses of water
sugar
1 glass white wine
1 glass port wine
25 strawberries
6 servings

Grate pineapple, add cold water, and strain through cloth to extract all possible juice. Or put pineapple in blender with water and strain. Add sugar to taste. Keep cool. When ready to serve, add white wine and port wine, and garnish with small pieces of pineapple and strawberries. Serve very cold.

288. RASPBERRY PUNCH (Ponche de Framboeza)

½ hour
4 cups raspberry syrup
1 bottle red wine
1 wineglass kirsch
4 slices pineapple, chopped
2 apples, peeled and diced
1 cup cracked ice
1 bottle soda water
15 servings

Mix first 6 ingredients and put in refrigerator. Just before serving add soda water. Serve in punch cups.

289. DELICIOUS STRAWBERRY MARQUIZETTE
Mar-keez-et' (Marquizete de Morango)

25 minutes
1 bottle champagne
1 bottle white wine
2 cups cut-up strawberries
1 bottle soda water
sugar
1 cup crushed ice
20 servings

Mix all ingredients with sugar to taste and serve over crushed ice in crystal champagne glasses.

290. PAULISTA PUNCH (Ponche Paulista)

25 minutes
1 cup vanilla ice cream
½ cup maraschino
½ cacao liqueur
½ cup brandy
1 bottle champagne
1 cup finely chopped oranges, pineapple, and strawberries
10 servings

Beat ice cream with maraschino, cacao liqueur, brandy, and champagne. Mix with chopped fruit and serve in small glasses.

291. FOAMING MILK (Leite Espumante)

10 minutes
4 glasses iced milk
4 tablespoons sugar
4 tablespoons cacao liqueur
1 cup crushed ice
4 to 6 servings

Mix first 3 ingredients together, beating very well, and serve over crushed ice.

292. FRUIT COCKTAIL (Coquetel de Ameixa)

10 minutes

½ cup gin
½ cup sherry
⅓ cup prune juice
⅓ cup orange juice
crushed ice
4 servings

Shake all ingredients together and serve with crushed ice.

293. STRAWBERRY COCKTAIL (Coquetel de Morango)

15 minutes

1 cup cleaned strawberries
2 cups orange juice
3 tablespoons whiskey
4 tablespoons crushed ice
12 servings

Separate 6 strawberries, put remainder through sieve or in blender. Add orange juice, whiskey and ice. Shake well and serve with half a strawberry in each glass.

294. SÃO PAULO COCKTAIL (Coquetel Paulista)

15 minutes

3 egg yolks, well beaten
1 cup cacao liqueur
1 cup port wine
1 cup cream
1 cup crushed ice
nutmeg
8 servings

Mix egg yolks with liqueur, wine, cream, and ice. Shake well. Serve with a dash of nutmeg in each glass.

295. Smiles Cocktail (Sorriso)

    15 minutes
  2 cups Calvados
  ⅔ cup gin
  2 tablespoons lemon juice
  ⅓ cup orange juice
  2 tablespoons grenadine
  2 tablespoons cream
  crushed ice
    8 servings

Mix all ingredients well, shake, and serve.

296. HILLBILLY COCKTAIL (Caipirinha)

10 minutes
grated rind of 1 lemon
sugar
lemon juice
cachaça or rum
crushed ice

Mix lemon rind with enough sugar to give a sweet taste. Take equal parts of lemon juice and *cachaça* or rum. Sieve the lemon sugar into this. Serve it with a little crushed ice. You may leave out the sugared lemon peel if you wish.

297. COCONUT COCKTAIL (Batida de Côco)
Prepare one week in advance.

½ hour
1 big fresh coconut
cachaça, brandy, or rum
8 servings

Make a hole in the soft end of the coconut and pour off all the coconut milk. Insert a small funnel and pour in as much *cachaça*, brandy, or rum as it will hold. Let stand for at least a week and serve ice cold from shell.

298. CHRISTMAS PUNCH (Ponche de Natal)

   1 hour

   3 large apples, cut into pieces
   1 pineapple, cut into pieces
   3 peaches, cut into pieces
   1 pound grapes, cut in half and seeded
   1 bottle white wine
   ⅓ cup sugar
   ¾ cup Cointreau
   ¾ cup cognac
   2 bottles champagne
   2 bottles sparkling water
      25 servings

Mix the fruits with wine, sugar, and liqueurs and let stand in the refrigerator for about ½ hour. Just before serving, add the champagne and sparkling water. Serve cold.

299. THRIFTY PINEAPPLE DRINK (Refresco de Casca de Abacaxi)

Before peeling pineapple for any purpose, scrub the outside well with a brush, so that it is perfectly clean. After peeling, put peelings and core, or any bits that have been cut out of pineapple, in large bowl. For every pineapple add ½ cup sugar and cover all with water. Cover very well and leave for 3 days—*not in the refrigerator*. Strain through a cloth. The juice will be slightly bubbly. Chill and serve.

Christmas is the biggest festival of the year. The old Brazilian Christmas was almost exclusively a church festival, with a bountiful supper on Christmas Eve after the midnight mass. The children helped to set up the *presépio* (crèche), which still has its honored place in Brazilian homes. With northern European and even American influence, we have adopted the customs of many countries, and our homes are bright with Christmas trees and greenery. Our greenery is often some arrangement of beautiful tropical leaves and blossoms, and our Christmas tree is not the spruce which you use, but a variety of pine or cypress, often planted in a giant flowerpot and kept from year to year to be used again. School is out for the summer, and trains, buses, and planes are filled with people going to join family or friends, or to the cooler mountains, for the holidays. In Rio de Janeiro the main *avenida* is a dazzling sight at night, with the living trees bright with thousands of lights and a dramatic, more-than-life-size *presépio* set up in one of the central *praças* (squares). In our homes the kitchen is buzzing with activity, and the children wait for Papai Noel (Father Christmas) to come on Christmas Eve. Papai Noel, with his white whiskers, dressed in the usual bright red with fur trimmings, must feel a little warm. The children seem to see no inconsistency in his wintry apparel, or in the fact that he appears in so many places at the same time—in the shops and on the streets. Christmas Eve supper consists of Stuffed Turkey, Brazilian style (Recipe 98), sweets, and nuts; and in every household, rich or poor, is served the typical *rabanadas* (Recipe 300). This is bread soaked in a spicy mixture, fried and served hot, as a dessert. Wine is the usual accompaniment to the meal, with hot black coffee to finish. All the family is together for this most beautiful night.

CHRISTMAS EVE DINNER

Stuffed Turkey (Recipe 98)
Sarrabulho (Recipe 99)
White Wine Soup (Recipe 38)
Rabanadas (Recipe 300)
Brazil nuts, raisins, dates, dried figs
Christmas Punch (Recipe 298)
Demitasse

Mother's Day has come to be celebrated in Brazil as in your country, on the second Sunday in May. Homes are decorated with flowers and a heart-shaped cake is baked for Mother (Recipe 301).

In Brazil, the month of June is a month of festivities. Although the traditional June parties are disappearing from the larger cities, principally in the south of the country, in the north, and in the interior, there are thirty days of fun and dancing.

St. Anthony's Day is on June 13, and originated in Portugal. This is the day when unmarried girls appeal to St. Anthony, who is especially clever at making matches. At midnight the girls make *sortes* to find out whom they will marry. One of the most popular *sortes* is dropping candle wax into a glass of water, where it takes various shapes, which with a little imagination will resemble a ship, plane, violin, etc., indicating the profession of the future husbands. Girls wearing white veils go to church to kneel contritely and ask the kind saint to give them their dearest wish, a good husband. At the church doors it is customary for beggars to ask for "saints' alms." St. Anthony is popular and beloved. The folk song runs:

"In my prayer I asked dear St. John
To give me a wedding ceremony.
St. John said no, St. John said no,
You must ask St. Anthony.
For matrimony, for matrimony, you must ask St. Anthony."

St. John's Day is the 24th of June. In Bahia it is especially important, and the hospitable Bahiano invites any stranger who may be passing his house to enter and partake of the traditional Mungunzá (Recipe 305), a pudding made of hominy, and *licor de genipapo*, a liqueur made of the genipap fruit. In Bahia, as well as in other parts of Brazil, the parties are held at night outdoors in the garden, which is decorated with hundreds of little colored paper flags strung on wires running between the trees and fluttering gaily in the breeze. There will be a great bonfire, because St. John's Night is supposed to be the coldest of the year. The young people dress in typical "interior" style, the girls in full skirts and flowered materials, full blouses snowy white and stiffly starched, and large straw hats. They dance around the bonfire, which burns all night, to the music of accordions, mandolins, and guitars. Sweet potatoes are roasted in the fire and eaten, soft drinks are served, and sometimes *cachaça* warms you up and makes you merry. When the clock strikes twelve, there is the traditional jump over the fire. Two young people, hand in hand, jump over the fire and thus become *compadres* (bosom pals) or lifelong friends. Prayers and *sortes* make this an occasion of fun and beauty. The colder the weather, the more beautiful the night, with bonfires, lighted balloons, and rockets and fireworks in the skies.

"The balloon is rising, the dew is falling,
The sky is so beautiful and the night is so good.
St. John, St. John, light a bonfire in my heart."

Refreshments for St. John Party

Quentão (Recipe 306)
Baked sweet potatoes
Cooked or baked green corn
Mungunzá (Recipe 305)
Pé de Moleque (Recipe 266)
Pumpkin Sweets (Recipe 268)
Cocadas (Recipe 261)
Demitasse

St. Peter's Night on the 29th of June ends the festivities. It is a night of lights and dancing and is the prettiest *festa* of them all. The sky is bright with fireworks; balloons mingle with the stars. Children try to catch the balloons as they fall.

They sing:
"Please fall, balloon, please fall, balloon, right here into my hand."
The balloon replies:
"I will not, I will not. I am afraid of being caught."

Sweethearts Day, on the 12th of June, corresponds to your St. Valentine's Day, and is the day when sweethearts, as well as husbands and wives, exchange presents and celebrate with flowers and a special cake baked for tea (Recipe 307). A clever wife or sweetheart will bake a beautiful heart cake, decorated with sugar or natural flowers, or make other favorite dishes to please her loved one. The reader might find some Brazilian recipe to try on that day, selecting one that she knows will appeal to the particular tastes of the gentleman—the Parmesan Chicken (Recipe 95) or Shrimp Pudding (Recipe 71), or one of the delicious fish recipes, prepared with stuffing or wine and oysters (Recipes 50 and 61).

Since Brazilians love festive occasions and family get-togethers, here are a few more menus to help you in planning a Brazilian *festa*.

FAMILY-GET-TOGETHER DINNER

Fruit Cocktail (Recipe 292)
Stuffed Suckling Pig (Recipe 106)
Farofa (Recipe 56)
Baked sweet potatoes
Fluffy Rice (Recipe 137)
Spinach Pudding (Recipe 160)
White Manjar with Prunes and Coconut (Recipe 215)
Demitasse

BRAZILIAN FEIJOADA DINNER (*feijoada* is a dish made of black beans)

Hillbilly Cocktail (Recipe 296)
Brazilian Black Beans (Recipe 142)
Fluffy Rice (Recipe 137)
Farofa (Recipe 56)
Peeled and sliced oranges
Fruit Salad (Recipe 238)
Demitasse

BIRTHDAY OR FIRST-COMMUNION FESTA

Decorated Cake (Use Recipe 301 with ornamental frosting)
Ham and Asparagus Canapés (Recipe 11)
Salad Shells (Recipe 16)
Churrasquinhos (Recipe 19)
Shrimp Sandwich (Recipe 27)
Brazilian Empadinhas (Recipe 81)
Cornstarch Butter Cookies (Recipe 172)
Quindins with Cheese (Recipe 180)
Almond "Hams" (Recipe 249)
Brazil-nut Bonbons (Recipe 257)
Coconut and Pineapple Balls (Recipe 273)
Mother-in-Law's Eyes (Recipe 270)
Soft drinks and orange juice for children
Copacabana Punch (Recipe 286) for grown-ups
Demitasse

Small Afternoon Tea with Family or Friends

Fresh Orange Cake with whipped cream (Recipe 165)
Hot buttered toast
Tongue Sandwich (Recipe 28)
Hot or iced tea
Hot coffee and milk

Holiday RECIPES

300. CHRISTMAS RABANADAS (*rah-bah-nah'-dahs*)

45 minutes

- 2 cups milk
- 2 tablespoons sugar
- 2 tablespoons port wine
- 3 egg whites, stiffly beaten
- 3 egg yolks
- 8 slices white bread
- 1 cup cooking oil
- 2 cups sugar
- 2 tablespoons cinnamon
- 2 pinches salt
  8 servings

Mix the cold milk with the sugar and wine, in a deep dish. Beat the egg whites stiff, add yolks, and continue beating. Soak the slices of bread in the milk, sugar, and wine mixture, leaving them for a few minutes. Dip each slice in the beaten eggs, sauté in the hot oil, turning to brown on both sides. Remove to absorbent paper. Mix the sugar with cinnamon and salt. Cover the bottom of a wide ovenproof plate with part of the sugar and cinnamon. Place the slices on the plate, and cover them with the remaining sugar and cinnamon. Serve immediately, or keep warm in the oven until ready to serve.

301. MOTHER'S CAKE FOR MOTHER'S DAY (Bôlo de Mamãe)

  1½ hours

  1½ cups butter
  3 cups sugar
  6 egg yolks, beaten
  1 cup milk
  1 cup coconut milk
  4 cups flour
  2 teaspoons baking powder
  10 egg whites, beaten
  20 servings

Cream butter and sugar, add yolks, and beat well. Mix milk and coconut milk, add it alternately with the flour and baking powder sifted together. Last, fold in beaten egg whites. Bake in a greased and floured deep round 9-inch pan or a large tube pan 50 minutes to 1 hour. Frost with ornamental frosting. You may use your own favorite recipe, but here is the one I use.

NOTE: Fine granulated sugar is used in this recipe, but put it through a very fine wire sieve first.

First part:

  7 heaping tablespoons sugar
  2 egg whites, beaten stiff
  1 tablespoon lemon juice

Add sugar gradually to the beaten egg whites, beating all the time. The sugar will dissolve and become perfectly smooth. Add lemon juice, beat again. Spread this frosting over the entire cake, reserving some for decorating, smoothing it on with a spatula. Leave it to dry.

Second part:

  1 egg white
  2 tablespoons lemon juice
  2 tablespoons water
  1 teaspoon vanilla
  4 cups sugar

Mix unbeaten egg white with lemon juice, water, and vanilla. Add sugar a little at a time, and knead with the hands until all sugar has been absorbed. Spread over cake, smoothing until it is like marble. Add 4 more tablespoons of sugar to the frosting described in the first part, put in pastry bag, and decorate cake with elegant arabesques.

302. COPACABANA CUP

To serve with cake on Mother's Day.

> 45 minutes
>
> 1 cup white grapes, seeded
> 1 cup chopped fresh or canned pineapple
> 1 cup chopped apple
> 1 cup strawberry syrup
> crushed ice
> 1 bottle white wine
> 10 servings

Mix fruit and strawberry syrup together and put it into the refrigerator for at least 2 hours. When ready to serve, put some crushed ice in the bottom of each glass, put in a good full tablespoon of the fruit mixture, fill up with wine.

Four recipes for the June festivities. These would be appropriate for use on your Halloween, which is similar in spirit to our June holidays, with fortunes, bonfires and informal fun.

303. SWEET-POTATO AND COCONUT CAKES (Balas de Batata Doce)

> 1½ hours
>
> 1 grated coconut
> 2½ cups cooked and mashed sweet potatoes
> 4 cups granulated sugar
> 4 tablespoons cocoa
> crystallized sugar
> 36 cakes

Put all ingredients except crystallized sugar in a heavy saucepan to cook, stirring constantly with a wooden spoon until the bottom of the pan can be seen and the mixture is thick enough to form into small balls. Roll each ball in crystallized sugar.

304. SWEET POPCORN (Pipoca)

¾ hour

1 cup sugar
1 cup corn syrup
6 tablespoons melted butter
10 cups popped popcorn
    15 servings

Boil sugar and corn syrup until hard ball is formed when tried in cold water. Add butter and pour over popped corn, mixing well. Form into 2-inch-thick roll and cut into 1-inch slices.

305. MUNGUNZÁ (*moon-goon-zá*)

2 hours

4 cups milk
3 cups cooked hominy
1½ cups sugar
stick cinnamon
¾ cup coconut milk
½ cup crushed peanuts
1 teaspoon salt
¼ cup tapioca
    8 large servings

Cook the milk, hominy, and sugar, with a piece of stick cinnamon, in a heavy kettle over a very low flame for about 45 minutes. Add coconut milk and crushed peanuts and cook for 45 minutes more. Add salt and tapioca and cook until tapioca is clear. It should be of a creamy consistency. If you are in a hurry and do not have coconut milk available, put a cup of shredded coconut in with the milk, hominy, and sugar.

306. QUENTÃO (*ken-town'*)

15 minutes

4 glasses *cachaça* or rum
4 slices lemon
1½ glasses water
4 cloves
6 sticks cinnamon
sugar to taste
10 servings

Mix all ingredients in a pan and bring to boil. Serve hot in china or earthenware cups.

307. SWEETHEARTS' CAKE (Bôlo do Querido)

A rich cake baked in the shape of a heart and frosted with the favorite frosting of your dearest sweetheart is a good way to win your way to *his* heart.

1 hour 15 minutes

2 cups sugar
1⅔ cups butter
8 egg yolks
6 tablespoons brandy
2½ cups flour
1 teaspoon baking powder
4 egg whites, stiffly beaten
bread crumbs
12 servings

Beat sugar and butter until creamy, add yolks, one at a time, beating all the time, and alternately add brandy and flour, to which the baking powder has been added. Last, fold in the stiffly beaten egg whites. Grease a deep, heart-shaped baking dish, flour it, and sprinkle some very fine dry bread crumbs *only on the bottom*. This will help in removing the cake from pan. Bake for 50 minutes at 375 degrees. Frost with any preferred frosting. If you have no heart-shaped pan, you may make it in a deep round pan or tube pan and decorate as you wish.

INDEX